A YEARN TO DISCERN

Finding Purpose and Fulfillment through Discernment

R. L. MACO

Copyright © 2020 by R. L. Maco

Published by Red Penguin Books

ISBN Print 978-1-949864-82-3

Digital 978-1-949864-83-0

All rights reserved.

No part of this book may be reproduced in any form or by any electronic or mechanical means, including information storage and retrieval systems, without written permission from the author, except for the use of brief quotations in a book review.

DEDICATION

This book is dedicated to the memory and legacy of my Beloved Sister, Alvina Rhea Johnson, whose ability to Discern was deeply clouded by her big heart and loving nature. When in doubt, Alvina always threw caution to the wind and led with her heart in all things personal. If we think about it, we all know and love, and perhaps, under-appreciate, an Alvina in our lives until it is too late. And if we think about it even more closely, we will notice how the ones with the biggest hearts are always the ones who get hurt the most in life.

This is why I also dedicate this book to all the Alvinas of the world. The world simply could not function without the Alvinas out there who open doors to the homeless, feed the hungry, clothe the poor and love without question, limits, judgment or condemnation. These are the people who make Hope a tangible reality instead of an obscure concept or fleeting moment.

It would be a huge disadvantage to our society if the Alvinas of the world conformed or turned in their big hearts even for a moment as we all know that our world can never have too much Love. In fact, our world is in desperate need of Love now more than ever before. And the Alvinas are always in a position to answer the call to display more love and compassion in any given situation. And even though their desire to show love and compassion is needed, it is my hope that the Alvinas of the world learn to not always lead *with their hearts and not always throw caution to the wind, but to Discern more in life so that their gift of love can be spread longer and wider throughout the world.*

And finally, I dedicate my knowledge of Discernment and my individual ability to Discern to all the Alvinas out there who believed and who continue to believe in humanity through their acts of love, faith, compassion and kindness, oftentimes to their detriment. It is my belief that we all enter into this world with unique gifts that we dare expose to this world for the betterment of civilization as a whole. And it is my forever Hope and Prayer that they, and that we all, learn to use, develop and cultivate our ability to Discern so that we can step into our destined greatest and change the world positively, the way it was specifically designed and intended for you, me and the human race. For I am convinced that this Hope and Prayer is a distinct possibility so long as we learn to develop and hone our ability to Discern in this forever-changing world.

CONTENTS

Introduction	vii
1. THE ORIGINS OF THE WORD 'DISCERN'	1
2. DISCERNMENT AND SPIRITUALITY	13
3. THE MEANING OF DISCERNMENT	27
4. WHAT DISCERNMENT IS NOT!	31
5. DISCERNMENT, CORE VALUES, PRINCIPLES & RULES	53
6. LIFE LESSONS THAT SHAPE YOUR ABILITY TO DISCERN	83
7. DISCERNMENT IN ACTION: DISCERNING SAVES LIVES	97
8. THE DISCERNMENT PROCESS	111
9. DISCERNMENT vs. INTUITION: IS THERE A DIFFERENCE?	119
10. PERSONAL DISCERNMENT	125
11. RELATIONSHIP DISCERNMENT	143
12. DISCERNMENT AND THE NICE-GUY SYNDROME	159
13. CHILDREN AND DISCERNMENT	167
14. PROFESSIONAL DISCERNMENT	177
15. DISCERNMENT IN THE AGE OF SOCIAL MEDIA AND UNACCOUNTABILITY	187
16. HOPE AND ULTIMATE DISCERNMENT	195
Notes	201
Acknowledgments	203
About the Author	205

INTRODUCTION

The word *Discernment* is neither a word that many of us use in our everyday vocabulary nor is it a word we think about to describe how we navigate life in times of conflict or in times of triumph. *Discernment* is a rather humble word; a humble word representing an important skill that works its magic best behind the scenes. Whether we know it or not, *Discernment* is often the unsung hero in our lives that helps us develop a clear path for how we view and value our lives, how we view the lives of others, and how we function in this unstable world. Being able to *Discern* helps us establish how we will allow ourselves to be treated and who we allow to influence our lives under what parameters.

Through my own self-reflection, I've learned that *Discernment* is a skill that many of us use without knowing or even understanding that it is the skill at work when we are operating at an optimal level. Just think about that for a second. When you are functioning at a purposeful and focused level, there are specific elements at work pointing you in the right direction to assist in the upward mobility of your life, your loved ones, the people in your circle and the world around you. One of those specific elements, and without a doubt, one of the most critical elements working on your behalf, is your individual ability to *Discern*, an ability that shouldn't be taken lightly by any means. And just like any other critical skill you should develop in life, the ability to *Discern* must be developed and put into daily practice in order for you to reap its benefits and rewards. Be mindful that the ability to *Discern* may come easier for some than others. However, with discipline and a more heightened consciousness of self, you can learn to *Discern* on an elevated level to ensure that you achieve a sustainable quality of life for yourself and your loved ones. This is true regardless of your physical state of being or other challenges you may be facing in life. Yes, the ability to *Discern* is that far-reaching if utilized and developed properly.

No matter what stage of life you are in, it is important to understand that *Discernment* is a staunch advocate for necessary change. Anytime you want to make positive and important changes in your life, no matter what those changes may be, you must initially look at self to determine what internal changes you will need to make first. You must also understand that changing YOU is the only change that is within your control. Therefore, on a personal level, if you really took some time to invest in honest, critical and vulnerable self-reflection, you'd realize that *Discernment* serves to implement changes while allowing us to accept and experience favorable outcomes in life. And for some of us, we are reaping these outcomes without even realizing how *Discernment* catapulted us to the victory. Quite frankly, when we achieve the desired result in any given situation, no one exclaims to themselves or to their friends, 'I did it! My ability to *Discern* got me through it!' On the contrary, once we achieve something great, we are eager to detail all the ways we believe the desired outcome was achieved. We may acknowledge all the people who helped make that outcome possible and then focus on what we did to make it happen. Unfortunately, no matter how much we'd pat ourselves on the back, we wouldn't acknowledge our individual ability to *Discern* or give *Discernment* the credit it's due for the role it played in the fruitful outcome. And depending upon the person, there may be several reasons why we don't look more introspectively to analyze exactly how we succeeded in the moment.

Even if we consciously analyzed the complete steps to our success in a particular situation, I can almost guarantee that we'd use every other possible word to describe our success without even considering the word *Discernment*; it's a shame, but it's true. But don't be too hard on yourself; most people don't focus on the behind the scenes steps that brought them to glory. It's just part of human nature for us to focus on the external or peripheral elements at work instead of the unique internal elements inside each and every one of us. And while all three elements, external, peripheral and internal, are important, the internal elements—which include the ability to *Discern*—is the ultimate safeguard that protects us at all times.

The good news is this: most humans possess the ability to *Discern* within us. Have you ever heard anyone say: 'everything you need in order to succeed is already inside you?' Well, guess what? They were right! That internal compass inside you is always on the job even when the other elements are not. And that's the beauty of the ability to *Discern*. Once you fully understand what it means and then learn how to *Discern* properly and consistently, you will further develop this critical skill and put it to use on a daily basis because it always works in your favor. Always! The problem with *Discernment* is the fact that most of us put it aside and simply do not use it. Unfortunately, when we do this, the skill becomes muted, ignored and undermined. And once the ability to *Discern* is silenced, other influences will quickly take over to dominate your actions. Although there are many influences that present themselves in the absence of *Discernment*, the biggest influence that drowns out the ability to *Discern* is one's emotions. And if you are leading with your emotions, you may as well be playing Russian Roulette with your life because you have now placed yourself on an unpredictable alleyway and you have no idea where it will lead.

What people fail to understand is this: just as knowledge is power, *Discernment* is Power with a Capital P because it involves the purposeful use of knowledge. In a nutshell, *Discernment* arms you with the power to take control over your life with clarity and focus. And on an even grander scale, *Discernment*, in many instances, takes you off someone else's path and places you on the path that was designed especially for you. And since *Discernment* is one of those unique internal elements that guide you in doing what's right for you, and often times, what's right for those in your circle and even beyond, it is high time for us to discuss the importance of *Discernment* and how mastering the skill of *Discernment* will change your life positively in many ways.

I want you to digest the fact that *Discernment* may very well be the culprit for most of the wise choices you've been making all along. How wonderful and unfortunate at the same time. Wonderful because you are operating at a high level of being that has propelled you, and hopefully anyone around you, to greater depths of consciousness and success. Unfortunate because even though *Discernment* is actively at work in your life, you have not acknowledged or even grasped the fact that it is at work. Therefore, you have not yet tapped into the full extent at which *Discernment* can enhance your life and elevate you to levels of success and completeness that you are, indeed, capable of achieving. However, because you haven't tapped into the full Power of *Discernment*, your mind probably has yet to imagine all that it can possibly accomplish. So what's the lesson here? Until you give the ability to *Discern* the opportunity to take on a pivotal role in how you navigate life, you will never give yourself the greatest opportunity to achieve your desired goals, objectives and purpose in life.

I cannot stress enough that the ability to *Discern* should never be underestimated. In fact, *Discernment* should be a foundational strategy used in your life on a continual basis. Whether at home, work, play, and during all other settings in-between, *Discernment* should be a skill that is used to constantly refine and/or redefine your life and the relationships you allow into your life. *Discernment* is meant to help uplift at all times. It is the gift that keeps on giving and it is imperative that it becomes a proactive partner in your life no matter what the situation is or who you are dealing with. The benefits of learning how to *Discern are endless*, particularly in today's global society laced with all the trappings of rapidly-changing technology, social media, changing morals, values, ethics and culture.

So with all this background in mind, the objective of this book is to explore the pertinent and life-changing components of *Discernment* so that you have a fountain or well from which to draw upon as you navigate through life's twists and turns. Through examples, exercises and by sharing some of my life experiences and lessons in *Discernment*, this book will explain in detail, why all human beings should invest time in developing the ability to *Discern* in order to achieve maximum fulfillment and true purpose in life. The objective of this book is to help you develop a strong ability to *Discern* so that you will reach your desired life goals.

We will begin our understanding of *Discernment* by acknowledging and discussing the roots/origins of the word '*Discern*' and then continue to build upon this initial discussion throughout the book. Through the concepts, principles, lessons, experiences and exercises, you should be able to understand what you need to do in order to begin *Discerning* effectively. And with that sentiment in mind, I wish you Happy *Discerning*!

Chapter One

THE ORIGINS OF THE WORD 'DISCERN'

CURRENT DEFINITIONS OF THE WORD '*DISCERN*'

How is the word *Discern* defined and where does the word *Discern* come from? There are several different definitions on the topic of *Discernment* or what I like to call 'modern-day definitions' used to define *Discernment*. These definitions vary slightly depending upon which sources you consult. If you open up any current dictionary, you will find that the most basic definitions of *Discern* include, but are not limited to, the following definitions:

1. 'the quality of being able to grasp and comprehend what is obscure'; 'an act of perceiving or *discerning* something.'[1]
2. 'the ability to obtain sharp perceptions or to judge well.'[2]
3. 'The ability to notice fine-point details; the ability to judge something well or the ability to understand and comprehend something.'[3]

In the Spiritual context, *Discern* has been defined as:

1. 'the ability to decide between truth and error, right and wrong.'[4]
2. 'a quality of attentiveness to God that, over time, develops into the ability to sense God's heart and purpose in any given moment.'[5]
3. 'Perception in the absence of judgment with a view to obtaining spiritual guidance and understanding.'[6]

All of these definitions are well and fine, and I am in agreement with most of them to a certain extent. However, these definitions do not dig deep enough and, therefore, fail to expound on the completeness of *Discernment* and what takes place when one is *Discerning*. Overall, these definitions fail to capture the true essence of *Discernment*, its unique properties and its true purpose and usage in daily life. Unfortunately, these definitions also do not capture the full extent of the power of *Discernment* and the role it plays in enhancing the quality of one's life. So let's first take a step back to uncover the roots of the word *Discern*.

THE ROOTS OF THE WORD '*DISCERN*'

The word *Discern* derives from the Latin word *Discernere* which means 'to separate, set apart, divide, distribute, distinguish or perceive.' The prefix *Dis* means 'apart' or 'off, away' and *Cernere* means to 'distinguish', 'separate', 'sift' or 'see certain'. The word *Discern* also comes from the late Fourteenth Century Middle English word *Discernen* which was borrowed from the Thirteenth Century Old French word *Discerner* which means to 'distinguish (between)' or 'separate (by sifting)'.[7]

Even further, an old-world translation of the word *Discern* defines *Discernment* as: "to perceive or recognize the difference or distinction between (two or more things); also 'distinguish (an object) with the eyes, see distinctly, behold'; also 'perceive rationally, understand.'[8]

Quite frankly, when you compare the origins of the word *Discern* to the more current definitions, you'll find that the current definitions of the word *Discern* do not do its origins justice. There are a number of keywords used in the initial definitions of the word *'Discern'* that should not be lost in today's translation or culture. Specifically, omitting such words as 'distinguish', 'distinct', 'sift' and 'set apart' from the current definitions tend to water down the in-depth meaning and function of the word *Discern*. My favorite word used in the original definitions of *Discern* is the word 'sift'.

'Sift' is defined as: 'to examine (something) thoroughly so as to isolate that which is most important or useful.'[9] Bingo! Using the word 'sift' makes perfect sense when describing the word *Discern* because you must understand that when you are *Discerning*, you are sifting through information in order to come to a rational decision. When you are *Discerning*, you are essentially deciphering through information that is readily available to you, and you must determine what information is salient and what information must be discarded. Even if you can imagine the physical act of sifting through something, the act of sifting underscores its relevance to the act of *Discerning*. What does this mean? Well, when you are sifting through something, you are looking for or trying to uncover something that is there, you just have to identify it. Sometimes what you are looking for is staring you in the face and other times it is less visible to you. But nevertheless, the information you need is there. But a very important aspect of *Discernment* is understanding that the information you need is not 'obscure', 'vague' or somehow intrinsically hidden from you. I'll explain this point by using the familiar idiom known as 'like looking for a needle in a haystack'.

DISCERNING VS. THE IDIOM "LIKE LOOKING FOR A NEEDLE IN A HAYSTACK"

Consider the popular phrase "like looking for a needle in a haystack." What does this phrase mean exactly? The phrase actually means this: the information you need is there but it is difficult or almost impossible to find. The salient part to keep in mind about this phrase is the fact that the information (needle) you seek is actually there or available. The phrase also makes you aware that, due to either the vastness of where the information is located coupled with the fact that you must sift through this vastness of information or, perhaps, the information you need to uncover is so subtle, it is difficult to ascertain. This idiom signifies that either the information itself is 'hidden', 'subtle', 'obscure' or 'vague' and, therefore, difficult to ascertain; or, the information is hidden within a vast location making it difficult to find. Either way, somehow, <u>the information itself is not easy to uncover</u>. Essentially, the information you need is somehow 'hiding' in a sea of information that makes it difficult to ascertain. That sums up this idiom succinctly.

However, this phase does not quite sum up how *Discernment* works because when it comes to *Discernment*, the difficulty in obtaining the information you need is totally dependent upon a person's individual ability to *Discern*, **<u>not because the information itself is 'hiding' or because the information is located in an obscure place or positioned in various places making it difficult to obtain</u>**. This is an extremely important point for you to comprehend. In other words, the difficulty in obtaining the information is not linked to the information itself, but rather, the difficulty lies with the person's individual ability to uncover the information. The level of difficulty has to do with a person's strong points or shortcomings; if a person's shortcomings dominate, then their ability to see information that is right in front of them will be blocked. Therefore, a person's ability to *Discern* is quite personal and will vary from person to person. Overall, the strength of that ability will determine whether the person will see the information that is, indeed, available to them.

A person must acknowledge that their individual ability to *Discern* is intimately connected to whatever is going on in the person's life that may or may not allow them to *Discern* in a particular situation or situations. This ability will also be connected to the person's character, personality and other unique traits of the person. We will discuss this point in more detail in the Chapter entitled Personal *Discernment*. However, the important point to remember is that *Discernment* takes place in the face of known facts and information you have at your disposal; this information is not designed to be difficult to uncover. And notice that when referring to this information in the context of *Discernment*, I have not used the word 'find'. I intentionally omitted use of this word when discussing *Discernment* because when you are *Discerning*, the information you need is not 'lost' or 'hiding' in the first place, so there's no need to 'find' it. The information simply exists and you have to identify it. This is why the 'needle in the haystack' analogy does not coincide with *Discernment* because with *Discernment*, the information you need is not 'obscure' or 'hidden' from you. If you are unable to absorb the information, it is because <u>YOU</u> failed to see it and that's all on you, not the information. The fact of the matter is, the information was conveyed to you either in writing, verbally and/or non-verbally and oftentimes, it is a combination of some or all types of such information. The failure to take heed of that information must be borne by the person receiving the information, not the information itself and not the person who conveyed the information to you.

One of the most crucial aspects of *Discernment* is the fact that it takes place in the face of known information. Understanding this fact is also why I personally take issue with those definitions of *'Discern'* that include the word 'obscure'. When something is 'obscure,' it is unclear, uncertain or unknown. However, when one is *Discerning*, they are not operating blindly to discover information that is unknown or unavailable to them. On the contrary, and as I will continue to state and demonstrate throughout this book, the act of *Discerning* takes place when information, particularly facts, are present; the information is readily available to the person. In other words, *Discernment* is not about trying to figure out a way through no way. Nope, that's not the case! Believe me, when you are *Discerning*, there is a way. And although there may be missing pieces of information, and also irrelevant pieces of information that you may have to sift through, the fact is, *Discernment* takes place when you have all the information you need to make the right choices and decisions in life.

There are so many times when we ignore information we receive because we are convinced that more information is needed before we can act. Unfortunately, we often use that stance as an excuse to continue with the status quo because it is easier to do nothing than to make waves; doing nothing does not require us to 'rock the boat' or implement necessary and hard-core changes. But if we are ready to

Discern and actually stay alert to what people are really communicating to us, we would understand that we were told exactly what we needed to know in order to make the right moves.

REFLECTIVE QUESTIONS: MISSED OPPORTUNITIES

I'd like you to take a few moments to reflect upon the following list of questions. Upon reflection, answer these questions that pertain to how you handled certain situations in the past. Take as much reflective time as needed before answering these questions.

1 - Can you recall any situation where you were provided with information about an opportunity that required you to make a decision in life but instead of taking advantage of the opportunity, you placed the information aside because you did not think the time was right for you to act? If so, please list each such opportunity(ies) that presented itself (themselves) to you?

_____

_____

_____

_____

_____

2 - Why did you decide not to take advantage of this opportunity(ies)? Were there other people (e.g., a partner, children, a parent, etc.) that played a role in your decision to turn down the opportunity(ies)? List all persons who you believe had an active or passive role in your decision to decline the opportunity(ies)?

_____

_____

_____

_____

3 - Perhaps you believe your particular circumstances (e.g., finances, recent divorce, demanding job, etc.), and not a person, played a role in your decision not to act on the opportunity(ies). Was your decision based upon your particular circumstances at the time? Please elaborate on the circumstances that you believe caused you to miss out on any opportunity(ies).

_____

_____

_____

_____

4 - Did you miss out on any opportunity(ies) due to both people and circumstances in your life at the time? Yes/No? If you feel both people and circumstances played a role in your decision, please elaborate on who and what prevented you from taking advantage of any opportunity(ies).

_____

_____

_____

_____

5 - Now that you have identified the persons and/or circumstances you believe influenced your decision to pass on an opportunity(ies) in life, please identify the specific reasons you used, at the time, to decline taking advantage of the opportunity(ies):[10]

_____

_____

_____

_____

_____

6 - How do you believe this missed opportunity(ies) could have changed your life if you took advantage of it? The change can be any type of change (negative or positive) you believe would have taken place had you taken advantage of the opportunity(ies) at the time. Please list each perceived change below.

_____

_____

_____

_____

Being honest when answering these questions is key. If you are honest with yourself, you will more than likely learn some things about yourself and you will reflect on who you were back then and who you are right now. Hopefully you will see a difference. Please do not be afraid of reflecting back on certain actions you took or did not take in life. <u>Reflection is critical for growth and personal development.</u> Perhaps there are significant changes you've made in life since then to now, or perhaps there is little change. This line of questioning is not about placing blame on anyone regarding the choices you made in life. It is, however, about understanding who you are, how you view the world, how you navigate relationships and how you handle life situations. After reading parts of this book, you may return to these questions with more answers to write down and maybe you will identify even more opportunities you declined in the past. The goal is for you to have a better understanding of why you declined any opportunities that presented themselves to you at some point in your life. In the end, the answers to these questions should act as a barometer for how well-developed or underdeveloped your ability to *Discern* was at that time. This is just the first step in a series of steps for you to take in developing your ability to *Discern* more readily.

DISCERNING ON A REGULAR BASIS

Here is an interesting fact that regular *Discerners* know and understand: in many instances, a person may communicate only ONE WORD, ONE PHRASE or even a SINGLE GESTURE, ACTION or LACK THEREOF that gives us a sufficient amount of information needed in order to make the right choices for ourselves. Friendships and intimate relationships are, perhaps, the best opportunities to take note of these brief encounters that give us pertinent information about a person; information which, in turn, tells us how to proceed with the person going forward. Dating is a great way to figure out certain things about people and ourselves in the process. Let's look at an example about dating to underscore this point.

The Dating Game

Let's say you are dating someone who uses swear words consistently when describing people he or she is not happy with. Do you realize this person is actually giving you insight into how they respond or react to people when they are upset with them? When this person conveys his/her stories of conflict to you, do not focus on what you're told the other person did because you are not privy to that person's side of the story. Who did what is actually irrelevant here because it's not your conflict to solve. What is relevant, however, is the fact that this person is calling another person outside of their name by using derogatory terms. What should cross your mind is, what would this person say about me if and when I make them upset? Again, if this person you are dating <u>consistently</u> refers to people they are upset with in unflattering terms, this is a valid question for you to ask yourself. A person who Discerns regularly may not need to hear this verbiage over and over again before making a rational judgment in their best interest. In addition, if this type of vocabulary does not sit well with you, then you should make it known to the person and see how they respond. If nothing changes on their end, then you are the one who needs

> to change either by limiting your contact with this person or by ceasing all contact with them altogether. It's your choice and it is clear that Discernment is calling your name for you to make appropriate decisions here.

When you are in the midst of *Discerning*, the information you will need in order to make sound decisions and proper choices is yearning for you to absorb and utilize appropriately, sometimes immediately depending upon the situation at hand. *Discernment* makes it possible for you to protect yourself and all who are affected by you. Understand that *Discernment* is about picking up your blueprint or roadmap and actually following it. It's not about tricking you or taking you through a series of mazes in order to find the correct path. When your sense of *Discernment* is at its peak, the path is clear to you the same way The Yellow Brick Road became clear to Dorothy in the *Wizard of Oz*. In other words, the path is brightly lit and waiting for you to follow it.

According to Buddhism and Kabbalah traditions, The Yellow Brick Road symbolizes what is known as The Golden Path. The Golden Path represents the path of the soul from egoism to enlightenment. Other definitions of The Yellow Brick Road define it as the road to success or happiness.[11] This is why the analogy between *Discernment* and The Yellowbrick Road makes sense because learning how to *Discern* leads to happiness and success. Learning how to *Discern* also forces you to drop your ego, pride and selfishness in order to follow the path of enlightenment. It all comes down to choice. We all make choices in life that will have lasting effects and consequences on our lives and the lives of others. If we actually took the time to understand why we're making these choices, we'd be more conscientious about making them. Being more conscientious would also help us realize that, often times, we make decisions and choices with emotions, pride and ego at the helm. Making choices under those circumstances only leads to regret, uncertainty and chaos, either immediately or eventually. This is why we need to be clear about when obscurity enters the picture and how our shortcomings are the source of such obscurity.

So when it comes to making appropriate choices, the only time obscurity comes into play is when you are NOT *Discerning*. This means that instead of seeing what is in front of you, you've become more preoccupied with other things that block your ability to see or comprehend what is right under your nose. In fact, the information is only obscure to the extent that one has failed to recognize the information available or, in many instances, specifically chooses to ignore it. But make no mistake about it, *Discernment* does not function on misinformation or unknown information. If there is one misconception about *Discernment* that must be dispelled, that is it.

So now that we discussed the origins of *Discernment*, in order to comprehend the full breadth of the word *Discernment*, it is necessary to break the word down to its simplest form so that we can understand what *Discernment* is truly all about. Once we understand what *Discernment* really means, we can then discuss and dissect different situations we experienced in life, situations where *Discernment* came into play, or should have come into play, during stressful, emotional, chaotic and also blissful times in our lives. *Discernment* is open to us for the distinct purpose of increasing our chances of success in confronting these situations. By analyzing the word *Discernment* in-depth, we will be able to understand where we went wrong in handling certain situations in the past as well as prepare ourselves to handle future situations that yearn for us to *Discern* in order to make it through the process successfully. By doing this, we will understand exactly how *Discernment* steers us in the right direction in the end, every time. So, let's next look at three foundational topics that are critical to your full understanding of *Discernment*:

1. *Discernment* and Spirituality;
2. The Meaning of *Discernment*; and
3. *Discernment*, Core Values, Principles & Rules.

Before you move on to the next segment, please review and analyze your answers to the questions you wrote down in this chapter. You should revisit these questions as needed. We will also answer more probing questions as you progress in your understanding of *Discernment*.

Chapter Two

DISCERNMENT AND SPIRITUALITY

If you ever ventured out to research books written on the subject of *Discernment*, you will find there are books that address *Discernment* in the Spiritual realm and then books that discuss *Discernment* in the secular context. Even essays or blogs you may find on the topic of *Discernment* are crafted in two separate categories: 1. *Discernment* and Spirituality; or 2. *Discernment* in everyday life situations. I've even come across writings that discuss *Discernment* as if it's a talent or gift that is received by some and not others. Some of these writings focus on the goal of finding out if YOU possess the gift of *Discernment* or not.

I find these positionings on the subject matter of *Discernment* to be problematic and conflicting. The notion that Spiritual *Discernment* and Everyday *Discernment* must be treated separately ignores the relationship between the two and how one affects the other. And furthermore, I find it reckless to discuss *Discernment* as if only a chosen few possess the ability to *Discern* as a gift or talent while others remain out of luck. This is not how *Discernment* works. Although I am in complete agreement that *Discernment* is a gift from God, it is a gift given to all of us, not a chosen few. Unfortunately, many of us fail to take advantage of this gift and therein lies the problem.

To be more specific, let's go back to the roots of the word *'Discern'*. In addition to the definitions of the word *'Discern'* discussed in Chapter One, it is no coincidence that the word *'Discern'* / *'Discernment'* is found throughout several books in the Bible, both in the Old and New Testaments. This is a significant fact to consider in your understanding of *Discernment*. The Holy Bible makes various references to *Discernment* with respect to understanding God, gaining wisdom, establishing truth and other biblical contexts surrounding the processing of information such as knowing right from wrong, good and evil, and the revelation of God. Throughout this book, I will consistently highlight an important fact about *Discernment that one should not forget*: *Discernment* is a God-Given internal element the same way Intuition is a God-Given internal element.[1]

The point to be made is that Spiritual *Discernment* begets Daily *Discernment* and ultimately flows into the same stream. The initial understanding of *Discernment* starts with the acknowledgment and acceptance of Spiritual lessons in *Discernment* and applying them to your everyday life in order to achieve clarity in understanding God, your life and your purpose in the world. In other words, both realms of *Discernment*, Spiritual and secular, are intimately connected. Therefore, it is misleading for one to discuss the Spiritual realm of *Discernment* and not discuss Daily *Discernment* and vice versa. Even worse, it is negligent for anyone to treat them separately as if one does not impact the other. That is a mistake you do not want to make.

The problem with discussing *Discernment* in the Spiritual context is that some people think you are only speaking to a certain segment of the population when you dare discuss God, Spirituality and the meaning of life. Some people will shut down immediately when you acknowledge the presence of God and God's hand in finding one's purpose. It would be preferable, and possibly sell more books, if this book spoke about God in a vague sense and solely used the word *'Spirit'* or *'Universe'* to discuss Spiritual *Discernment* and the role it plays in our lives. Some people would feel more comfortable if that's how I'd position any discussion of *Discernment* and Spirituality. However, I would be doing myself, the topic of *Discernment*, and anyone attempting to learn how to *Discern* properly, a disservice by not staying true to the source, the understanding, the power and the meaning of *Discernment*. Therefore, I simply will not do it.

The truth of the matter is, *Discernment* is not a comfortable topic to discuss and dissect. Anyone who wants to either learn how to *Discern* properly, improve upon their *Discerning* skills, or learn how to *Discern* more consistently, will need to understand *Discernment* entirely, and that includes acknowledging the source and strength of *Discernment*. One cannot be willing to accept only certain aspects of *Discernment* and think they will achieve maximum fulfillment in life. Therefore, understanding the source and, certainly, the Spiritual source of power that stands side by side with the ability to *Discern*, is a pivotal part of grasping its concept and being able to put it into practice effectively. Moreover, most humans possess the ability to *Discern*.[2] We actually start *Discerning* as children even though we do not know that's what we are doing. I will discuss Children and *Discernment* in a subsequent Chapter, but you should know that, absent neurological or developmental disabilities, we all begin *Discerning* early in life. But as we experience life more and more and our personalities and character traits settle in, we balk at *Discerning* as we allow people and things to influence our lives often times without even knowing it. Despite what we allow to get in the way, our ability to *Discern* is given to us with the intent that we use it to gain understanding and wisdom as we navigate life; *Discernment* was not meant to be used by only a chosen few.

LIVING BY THE GOLDEN RULE

The best example I can give to reinforce the relationship between *Discernment* and Spirituality is to discuss The Golden Rule. Just in case you don't know what The Golden Rule is, it is the Rule that you treat people the way you want them to treat you. This Rule may be found in more than one source, but it is firmly established in the New Testament of the Holy Bible. Luke 6:31 states "And as you wish that others would do to you, do so to them."[3] Matthew 7:12 states it similarly as follows: "So whatever you wish that others would do to you, do also to them, for this is the Law and the Prophets."[4]

Now, while I'm willing to bet that some people would find issue with the source of this Rule, let us stay focused on its meaning and how its application to your life will change your perspective and allow you to see and approach interactions with people differently going forward.

THE SIMPLICITY OF THE GOLDEN RULE

The premise behind The Golden Rule is quite simple: treat people the same way you would want them to treat you. If we all thought about this Rule before we spoke to someone, how differently would our words and actions be toward one another? Would we even approach someone under certain circumstances if we thought about this Rule first? Think about the fact that we all want to be treated with respect and dignity. Keeping that thought in mind, the question becomes, when we initiate interactions, especially when we approach someone to complain or criticize, do we approach everyone with the same respect and dignity we expect to receive in return? Also think about this: when we are met with anything less than dignity and respect, do we respond in a way that takes into account our actions or thoughts that may have precipitated a particular response from someone? Think long and hard about your answers to these questions for a moment. Sometimes it's the thought(s) we carry around in our minds about the person or situation we are approaching that dictates how we convey a message to them. I can recite two life situations that come to mind when thinking about the The Golden Rule and its application to daily life.

Life Situation # 1 - R.E.S.P.E.C.T!

When you hear Aretha Franklin sing the song 'R.E.S.P.E.C.T!', you can feel the intensity of the song and its power through every verse; you can even feel it in the inflection of Ms. Franklin's voice. The song and how she sang it struck a timeless chord with the country and the world, a chord that still resonates with the world today. There is a distinct reason why this song is identifiable to all. Why is that!? Well, as humans, we all have this innate belief that we should be treated with Dignity and Respect. However, and ironically enough, not all of us believe that we should treat others with the same Respect and Dignity that we all believe we deserve. And that posturing, ladies and gentlemen, summarizes the fundamental problem with humanity and, arguably, the primary reason for most, if not all, of the major and minor conflicts prevalent in the world today. Whether today's or yesterday's conflicts are tied to issues of religion, culture, politics, race, socio-economics, class, gender, or any other issues that we find permeating through one's oppression and violence towards another, when we strip down the issues to its meager beginnings, we will find that the basic issue underlying all other issues is the fundamental issue of Respect and Dignity or a lack thereof.

As humans, we all expect to be treated with Respect and Dignity. We should all know that respect is reciprocal, yet, we constantly find ourselves in situations where people are demanding our respect while treating us as less than deserving of respect. It's sad to say but there are a number of people who use their prejudices, social status, wealth, education, race and a whole host of other factors, as weapons for the primary purpose of denying others the fundamental human right of Respect and Dignity. And they do this while simultaneously believing that they should be automatically respected at all times. Anyone walking around with that attitude and belief system is dangerous. And unfortunately, many of us actually walk around with such an attitude.

Now here is the most interesting part of all this: if we all followed The Golden Rule, this problem of lack of Respect, along with the conflicts it creates, would be eliminated. Again, The Golden Rule is rather simple: I'll respect you and you respect me. This Rule does not take into account anything other than the fact that we are all human beings, that's it. It doesn't take into consideration your race, gender, ethnicity, sexual preference, education, culture, social status or anything else. If we were to take into account anything other than the <u>common denominator</u> that we are all human beings, we now enter that slippery slope of leaving the realm of objectivity and entering the realm of subjectivity. The fact that we are all human is the one and only fact we share together; it is our universal connector. No other fact applies to all of us besides the fact that we are all human. In other words, the fact that we are all human is the only fact you need in order to treat everyone with Respect. Any other facts are distractors, that is, information used subjectively to uplift some and *alienate others. I'll tell you that adding subjective considerations onto The Golden Rule only serve to validate some at the expense of others. Put simply, adding more information onto the fact that we are all human is a flawed response that one uses when they're hurting on some level, whether they know it or not; in turn, they project that hurt onto others. This is irresponsible on so many levels.*

However, if we leave the subjectivity out of the equation, and, therefore, choose to Discern, we would use The Golden Rule and take into account the only two relevant pieces of information that make up this Rule, which is the following:

We are all human, and

All human life should be treated with Respect and Dignity.

That's it folks! All you needed to know to process and implement The Golden Rule is the fact that we're all human, so let's respect one another. Some of us fail to understand that giving another human being respect should be done so without any strings attached, especially strings that are attached due to a perceived social status used to prejudge and condemn another's life.

Do you understand how we could change the world just by simply following this Rule in our daily lives?! This is a Rule that flows from the Spiritual realm and is cock full of lessons in *Discernment*. But for some people, including those who are in positions of authority and power, this Rule will never be incorporated into their daily lives because it is not a part of their belief system. Said differently, some people start with the mindset that not everyone is deserving of respect. As a result, these people will continue to encounter and/or create negative and life-threatening situations when they encounter others due to their behavior and overall thought-process. The thought-process I'm referring to is the incredulous belief that certain human lives are more valuable than others. Let's provide a scenario to make this point more tangible. For example, if you believe that I, as a female, am not deserving of respect because of my gender, your thought-process will dictate that you will not treat me with respect no matter what I say or do if we have an encounter. Such a thought-process is tragic. In fact, I find no other thought-process more dangerous than this one. And on a global scale, persons with such mindsets create and implement policies that has caused and will continue to cause the senseless death of millions. This is why our world will continue to experience unnecessary conflict and strife that will be perpetuated from generation to generation. This type of mindset and belief system, my friends, is about as far away from *Discernment* as you can possibly get.

THE KEY TO UPHOLDING THE GOLDEN RULE:

<u>The Golden Rule Places the Onus on Each of Us to GIVE Respect FIRST with Each Encounter! The Respect You Give Is Not Premised Upon Someone Earning or Deserving Your Respect</u>

Here is why you should follow The Golden Rule: The most important aspect of The Golden Rule, and the one aspect of the Rule that most people do not comprehend, is the fact that your implementation of this Rule requires that you give Respect to EVERYONE because you want EVERYONE to treat you with Respect. In other words, the Rule places the onus on YOU to be proactive and approach each person you encounter with Respect because that is how you would want others to approach you. The giving of Respect is not dependent upon the other person showing Respect towards you first. Rather, the Respect you give is solely dependent upon your expectation of being treated with Respect…..YOUR expectation, not anyone else's expectation or perception of you.

The Rule, however, does not guarantee that your expectation will be fulfilled with each person you encounter. Keep in mind, the Rule does not state: 'Respect People Who Respect You!' Or 'Respect People Who Earn Your Respect!' Nonetheless, The Rule does require that your Respect be given to people because you have an expectation that people will Respect you. *It's an expectation that you must maintain despite the fact that some people will never approach you with Respect.* As unnatural as that may sound and as difficult as it may be to implement, this is necessary because by acting in this manner, the Rule allows you to be in control of your emotions and in control of each situation you encounter. Furthermore, your offerance of Respect will not be dependent upon another person's moods, bias, prejudice or negativity that they may bring to you. Instead, you will GIVE Respect PROACTIVELY because as an enlightened person, you will continue to expect to receive Respect and even if you do not receive it from someone, you will not respond in kind because you will not succumb to someone else's behavior and disposition in life. Remember, you are a *Discerner*. Therefore, you will continue to conduct yourself in a respectful manner until you are able to remove/disengage yourself from the person acting disrespectfully towards you. Because if you dispense with the Rule during an encounter and you withhold Respect due to the lack of Respect or outright disrespect displayed by another towards you, you give that person control over you during that encounter. And now your response will include an emotional element that may change the course of the encounter and possibly your life. Think about it. In any given situation, all it may take is one emotional response to what you perceive as another's disrespect towards you and your life can be changed forever. If you dispense with the Rule and place your emotions in charge, a life-altering change is a distinct possibility you may face. However, if you are *Discerning*, you will uphold The Rule, a Rule that is not dependent upon anyone else except YOU. The application of the Rule does not change with each person you encounter. On the contrary, the application is uniformly applied to everyone. The Rule requires you to expect to receive Respect in return. In order to do that, you must be hopeful that your encounters with people will be respectful. Keeping 'Hope' at the forefront of this Rule is crucial. We will discuss the advantages and significance of keeping 'Hope' at the forefront of your actions side by side with *Discernment* and how doing so will elevate your way of life immensely.

Those people who do believe and follow The Golden Rule on a daily basis and learn how to avoid numerous negative encounters and conflicts are better able to handle the negative elements in life that seek to stump personal growth. They reap huge benefits, one of which is peace of mind while staying on the path to purpose and enlightenment. These are the people who will choose to stand on relevant facts when encountering a person who does not believe they are deserving of respect. These people use knowledge productively by not responding in kind; in fact, they will *Discern* that sometimes a response to a disrespectful person is not even required. Their response is one of disengagement instead of escalation. But no matter what their response is, their response, if any, will be led by their ability to *Discern* and will keep them on the right track and in control of their actions and emotions.

REFLECTIVE QUESTIONS: RESPECT & THE GOLDEN RULE

1 - As a general rule, do you believe in following The Golden Rule? Why or why not?

_____

_____

_____

_____

_____

2 - If you do follow The Golden Rule, do you automatically apply this Rule when you interact with all strangers (e.g., the general public)? Yes/No?

_____

3 - If your application of this Rule is not automatic, do you give respect to people in general based upon how you believe others treat you first? In other words, is the respect you give to strangers dependent upon the respect, or lack thereof, that you feel they display towards you? Yes/No? Please elaborate on your basis for giving respect to others.

_____

_____

_____

4 - Is there another principle you follow that influences how you treat others you meet or interact with (excluding friends, family, co-workers and others you interact with frequently)? Yes/No? If yes, what is the rule or principle you apply when interacting with people in general?

5 - Can you recall the reason why you adopted this rule or principle?

6 - Do you remember when you were first introduced to this rule or principle that you follow consistently? Were you taught this rule/principle as a child and continued to follow it because you were raised to follow it?

7 - If you were not taught this rule/principle as a child, did you consciously follow this rule/principle through your own revelation or by way of education as an adult? Yes/No? Elaborate on why you decided to follow this rule/principle as a guiding principle in life?

_____

_____

_____

_____

_____

Once again, think and reflect upon your life and any experiences that come to mind before answering the reflective questions.

So now let's dig a little deeper into the issue of Respect. Have you ever given thought to the fact that what you may have perceived as disrespect may not necessarily be considered disrespect from the other person's perspective? Let's discuss an example with less catastrophic consequences than the example above, but will also help us understand *Discernment* and Spirituality much better.

Life Situation # 2 - After you, My Dear

As someone from Generation X, I am realizing more and more that a number of young millennials do not necessarily open doors for me with the same consistency that individuals from my generation, and the generation before mine, open doors for me. By no means am I saying that all millennials do not open doors, but I have noticed that a number of millennials I come across do not. Now, as a woman of a certain age, I freely admit that there is a part of me that expects a man to open the door for me because that is what I've been used to all my life. Needless to say, I am a creature of habit, as we all are, and having a door opened for me is one of those habits I've grown accustomed to. I am entering my fifth decade on this earth and I can literally count on one hand how many times a man from my generation has not either opened a door for me or allowed me to enter or exit an elevator first, because rarely does that happen.

Nonetheless, in the off chance that a man does not open the door for me or wait until I enter or exit an elevator, regardless of his age, color or any other characteristic, I do not get upset with him over it. Why? For me, the reason is very simple: I start with the cold hard fact that no one is obligated to open the door for me. That's a fact! Now of course, I can interject into the story that opening a door for someone is the polite or courteous thing to do. I may also believe that opening a door for someone is an indication of one's upbringing. But understand that such information is subjective and distracting only. The reality is that no one is obligated to open the door for me. Therefore, if a man does not open the door for me and he's not obligated to do so, why would his failure to open the door immediately translate into him being disrespectful towards me or, worse, mean that he can't stand women or that he somehow has an issue with me personally? Why does it have to be seen as a negative because someone failed to open the door for me? Maybe the person was preoccupied at that moment. Maybe the person was not taught to do that. Or maybe the person tried to open the door for a woman one time and was met with a response that he didn't have to open the door. I have no idea why he didn't open the door for me and it's not my job to condemn him because he didn't do so. Focusing on what this man failed to do only preoccupies my mind with negative thoughts. In other words, it serves no purpose and, therefore, I refuse to allow such thoughts to breathe or take up residency in my head. Someone failing to open a door for me is not automatically synonymous with someone disrespecting me.

What I do know is that if I later saw the same man directly behind me as I began walking through a door, I would still open the door for him because I will not dispense with my commitment to following The Golden Rule just because he may not be following the same Rule. I do this because me following this Rule actually frees my mind because it ensures that I don't focus on irrelevant information. Instead, it allows me to be in control of my emotions and actions and not allow myself to be preoccupied by someone else's actions. I am insistent upon not allowing anyone to stop me from upholding my principles just because they did something that I may have misinterpreted. Or to take it a step further, why should I alter my course just because someone *doesn't believe the same things I believe? For all I know, this man may very well uphold The Golden Rule and just had a bad day. Here's the thing, we all make choices in life. We can choose to allow other people's actions to create negative thoughts in our head that distract us from being who we are and, therefore, change our focus to some insignificant matters that do not serve any positive function in our existence except to judge, condemn and form prejudices against one another; or we can stay the course and not be shaken by circumstances we happen to encounter. How dare we allow our circumstances to dictate our future! All this because of one person's actions that you are second-guessing to begin with. That makes no sense.*

The other, and more appropriate, choice in this type of situation would be to stay committed to upholding The Golden Rule. By sticking to The Golden Rule, you will exude confidence and will continue on a particular path that will also keep you in control of the outcome of your daily interactions even when others do not uphold the same values, principles, ethics, morals and beliefs. Even better, you will limit the amount of distractions, particularly emotions, that tend to take over the situation and lead you astray by prompting you to react emotionally to what you perceive as a negative encounter. Clearly, the choice of sticking to your principles is one of Discernment and that is the side you want to be on during these situations.

The point I am making is that the Spiritual realm is always providing you with lessons, rules and principles that you should use in your daily life no matter who you are interacting with, where the interaction is happening or the context of the interaction. Also, keep in mind that someone failing to open a door for you is a very small matter in the grand scheme of life encounters. On the other hand, the broader issue of giving and receiving Respect to human beings is a bigger lesson in *Discernment* that if you fail to grasp, may result in more hefty consequences for you and those around you. This is why your goal is to *Discern* on a regular basis. But in order for you to handle the big and more complex lessons in *Discernment* like Respect and Human Dignity, you need to be able to identify and handle the small *Discernment* lessons first, like someone not opening a door for you.

We will discuss Respect when dealing with people you know and interact with continuously in subsequent chapters. But first let's understand your treatment of others in society and whether that treatment is conditioned upon subjective standards in some way.

The bottom line is this: looking at *Discernment* in the Spiritual context as separate and apart from *Discernment* at work, *Discernment* on vacation, *Discernment* in familial relationships, and all other daily situations where the opportunity to *Discern* arises, is a grave mistake that you must correct now so that you will be in a position to handle other, more crucial lessons in *Discernment* when it matters most.

Chapter Three

THE MEANING OF DISCERNMENT

Let's be clear, *Discernment* is about Enlightenment. *Discernment* is also about making informed judgments and hard decisions. *Discernment* is about being perceptive, rational, objective, logical and forward-thinking, to name a few things. And, yes, *Discernment* requires you to discriminate, oftentimes within seconds, depending upon the situation you are faced with. But the ultimate goal of *Discernment* is to protect you from the pitfalls prevalent in life to which you may succumb when you are confronted by certain situations. If your ability to *Discern* is not properly developed or if it is not used at all when this happens, you may be headed for trouble, sometimes in more ways than one.

Discernment is also about guidance, fulfillment, purpose and direction. When you learn how to *Discern*, you set the stage to make sound judgments in the face of constant adversity and potential threats in life. *Discernment* seeks to move you forward in life, productively, with the steadfast purpose of improving your life and ultimately improving the world around you. Now these words provide the basis for a definition of *Discernment* that is a more functional and practical definition taking into account the roots of *Discernment*. *This definition* helps us understand better why *Discernment* is so important and what purpose it truly serves in life. So here is our new definition of *Discernment*.

> *Discernment*: Having the ability to sift through different types of information, constant adversity and potential threats in life while consistently making appropriate choices, rational judgments and proper decisions that will propel you forward with the steadfast purpose of improving one's life and ultimately improving the world around you.

The true intent of *Discernment* is to keep you and your actions in line with your ultimate path in life. *Discernment* is a navigation system that is superior to any other navigation system you will ever encounter. Not even your mother's wisdom can compete with *Discernment*. Do you know why? *Discernment* is about navigating your way in the midst of dealing with the daily chaos of life. While your mom can see the pitfalls of certain places you are venturing into based upon her experiences going down certain roads before you, your mother cannot know completely your path in life because her perspective, just like anyone else's perspective, is colored by her own experiences and perceptions of life and existence. And although your mother may be right 99.9% of the time, and she may know you better than anyone else, ultimately, she doesn't know what your true path in life is and cannot dictate your path in life unless you give her the power to do so. Sorry, mom; love you, but it's true. This is why self-reflection becomes an integral part in how well you will develop your ability to *Discern*. And if you put aside your ability to *Discern* only to go about your daily life allowing loved ones, or anyone else for that matter, to tell you what you're good at, what you should do, what job you should take, etc., you'll never get to the point where you clearly understand what your true purpose in life is meant to be.

Remember, each one of us is different; each of our lives marches to a different chaotic or symphonic rhythm, if you will. This is true whether we're talking about the chaos we're born into or the chaos we've created for ourselves. Therefore, if we all took time out, periodically, to understand ourselves, our past, our present and our future, we would be in the driver's seat of the path we are destined to blaze. No one else should be the author of that story except you and God.

So that you can appreciate the value of *Discernment* and place it into perspective, let me first inform you of the two (2) opposite ends of the *Discernment* Spectrum. By doing so, we can bring its relevance into sharp focus:

1. *At a minimum, understanding and learning how to Discern will allow one to take full advantage of prime opportunities that will present themselves, opportunities that will impact one's life for the better.*
2. *At a maximum, understanding and learning how to Discern can make the difference between one's life or one's death.*

Discernment Spectrum

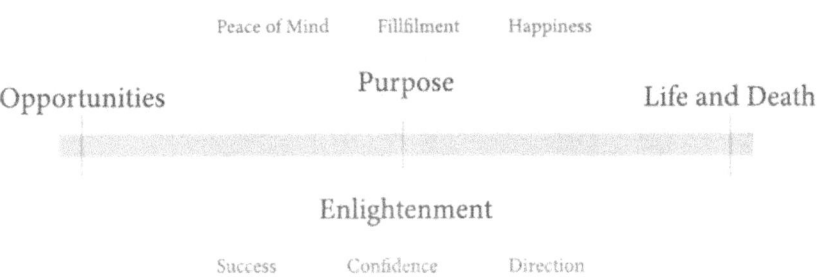

Now I know these are two stark contrasts at each end of the Spectrum, but knowing both ends of the *Discernment* Spectrum leaves little room for misunderstanding. What you'll find in-between these two ends of the Spectrum is peace of mind, confidence, enlightenment, truth, happiness and purpose. The bottom line is, no matter what end of the *Discernment* Spectrum you may find yourself at any point in life, using your ability to *Discern* always creates a win-win scenario. Once you realize and comprehend that the value and use of the ability to *Discern* results in a win-win scenario, you're on your way to true enlightenment. Acquiring this knowledge is the 'Ah Ha!' Moment and well-kept secret of *Discernment* which makes its relevance unmatched. No matter how you slice it, there is no competing with *Discernment* if you fully understand its unique qualities and the value of its *Power*. Once you do, you will apply it to every aspect of your life and finally see the positive results you've been expecting in life but haven't been able to achieve…until now.

So remember to always keep the meaning of *Discernment* at the front of your mind so that it may soothe you immediately when situations start to boil over and require you to think sharp. Remember, your actions and your future depend upon it. To sum it all up, *Discernment* is your ticket to upward mobility; don't leave home without practicing it.

Chapter Four
WHAT DISCERNMENT IS NOT!

At this point you should have a better understanding of what *Discernment* means and how it will change your life in numerous positive ways if you commit yourself to *Discerning* on a daily basis. But now that we know what *Discernment* IS, it would behoove us to learn specifically what *Discernment* IS NOT.

Understanding what *Discernment* IS NOT is also a key component to understanding when you are actually *Discerning* or when you are shooting in the dark. There are no negative components to *Discernment*. Please remember that. *Discernment* is about sifting through information, good and bad information, in order to make the appropriate decisions for your life, decisions that will protect you and yours, but decisions that will NOT require you to intentionally hurt others.

First and foremost, while *Discernment* requires you to make judgments, *Discernment* is not about making judgments for the purposes of condemning, degrading, demeaning, diminishing or devaluing another person in any way, shape or form. In addition, *Discernment* is not simply about being right or wrong or about mindlessly passing judgment or even about discriminating, although, on some level, judging and discriminating are important aspects of the process of *Discerning*.

However, judgment and discrimination are not the focus of what *Discernment* is all about. And understand this, *Discernment* is not about lifting yourself up by putting someone else down. On the flip side, this also means that *Discernment* does not involve lifting someone else up to the detriment of oneself. In other words, *Discernment* does not cause direct or collateral damage to someone else, including yourself. I cannot begin to tell you how important this piece of information is to your understanding of *Discernment*. There are so many people who miss this point and proceed to get themselves involved in situations they never should have entered into in the first place. So when I say *Discerning* will not lift you up while bringing someone else down, and vice versa, I am really saying that you need to pay close attention to the situation that has presented itself to you. Paying close attention is what *Discernment* is all about.

As you *Discern* through a situation, you must make an assessment of the facts that have been specifically presented to you so you can decide whether or not you should get involved. Similarly, if you are confronted with a situation where you must make an individual decision for you and/or your family and loved ones, *Discerning* will allow you to make the right decision and move forward in the correct manner. Either way, *Discernment* should be your navigation tool that guides you to your destination. When you are using *Discernment* as a navigation system, you will not need to second-guess whether the navigation system is utilizing the best route to get you to your destination.

In situations where someone presents you with a problem that needs to be solved, you will need to *Discern* whether or not this is your problem to begin with. If it is not your problem, then the question shifts to one of whether or not you should take on the problem in some way. I say this because some situations may be presented to you as if it's your problem to solve or to assist in solving, when, in fact, it is not your problem to get entangled with on any level. Therefore, being attentive and actually digesting the information relayed to you is paramount. And if we really dig deep into *Discernment*, your antennas should already be up when a person presents a problem to you as if it's your problem to solve when it is uniquely their problem, not yours. Hopefully, you will be able to *Discern* this initial fact before you even listen to all of the sorted details of their dilemma. Depending upon the person, you must proceed with extreme caution when dealing with a person who positions a problem to you this way because they are telling you so much about themselves. First and foremost, they are telling you that they are thinking solely about themselves and what they desire. Put simply, they are selfish. They are also giving you insight into how they will treat you if you get involved. Please be aware that they may potentially blame you if you get involved and something goes wrong or the problem is not solved after you get involved. Be aware that they may throw you under the bus if they feel it necessary. These are tried and true characteristics of selfish people. When selfish people position a problem this way, often times they are attempting to dump the problem on you; they don't even know they are telling on themselves and how selfish they are. But what's most important is that YOU know they are telling on themselves. This is *Discernment* at its finest. Let's use some examples to solidify this point:

Example 1: Not My Emergency!

> *A gentleman I worked with once taught me an important lesson. He said to me "an emergency on your part doesn't necessarily create an emergency on my part." This statement was life-changing for me. He was referring to a situation that a family member presented to him as an emergency and the person expected him to drop everything he was doing to attend to this so-called 'emergency' situation. After being told about this 'emergency', my co-worker informed me that no one's life or liberty was at stake, therefore, this was not a true 'emergency'. This was the first and most important point to understand, he said. In fact, the situation had to do with the person needing $300.00 by 6:00pm that day so that he could pay his cable bill. If he did not pay the bill by 6:00pm, his cable would have been turned off. This person pleaded with my co-worker and insisted that not only must he come up with the money, but that he*

needed to bring the money to him at the cable payment center where he was waiting to pay the bill.

That day, my co-worker was responsible for picking up his son from football practice by 6:00pm and since he got off work at 5:30pm, he would have just enough time to leave work and pick up his son on time. The only person he could have possibly called to pick up his son that day was his son's mother. Unfortunately, he had to consider three things: 1. He had joint custody with the child's mother, 2. today was his day to pick up his son and 3. he was barely on speaking terms with his son's mother. Due to these considerations, his son's mother picking up the child was out of the question. And finally, my co-worker did not have $300.00 anyway. He could potentially borrow the money from his mother, but his mother was on a fixed income and couldn't really afford to lend anyone money. But as a mother she would do it for him and my co-worker knew she would. Knowing his mother's situation, however, my co-worker believed that borrowing from his mother would be selfish unless it was done for an actual emergency. For my co-worker, an emergency meant he only borrowed money from his mother if he needed something for his son or unless his or a loved one's life and liberty were truly at stake. He told me, since this family member's situation did not fall within those parameters, he was not borrowing any money from his mother for this particular situation.

After providing me with all this information, my coworker politely informed me that as far as he was concerned, this was not a true emergency and it certainly wasn't <u>his</u> emergency. Therefore, he was not going to get involved. He called the family member and very nicely informed him that he could not help him out. He did not explain why he couldn't help; he simply informed the person that he was sorry but he was unable to assist him with his dilemma. It was now about 5:30pm so my co-worker bid me a fond farewell with a smile and proceeded to go pick up his son. He left worry free and in good spirits.

When my co-worker came into work the next day I asked him what happened to the family member's cable situation. He said to me 'I don't know; I told you yesterday, not my emergency.' He told me he didn't call the family member back yesterday after declining to get involved. My co-worker then explained to me that just because someone is having an 'emergency', that doesn't mean it's <u>your</u> emergency. He told me that having your cable turned off is not a life or death situation, it's a money management issue. He stated that a money management issue was someone else's personal problem and not his problem to get involved with nor was it his problem to solve. He said if the person wants the cable to stay on that bad, they will find a way. And if they don't, the cable being turned off will not cause anyone to die. He said he will not inconvenience himself, his son or his mother, because someone else cannot get their personal affairs in order. He told me he knows this person very well. If he gave him the money, the person will undoubtedly call him again and again every time he needs money to bail him out of these types of personal matters. He also revealed that the person already borrowed money from him previously that he hasn't paid back in 3 months like he promised. He reiterated that this man's personal affairs are not his problem. And guess what? Around lunchtime that day, my co-worker informed me that the family member called to let him know he was able to get the money to keep the cable on without his assistance. And then my co-worker looked at me and said, "I knew he would find a way to keep his cable on. Always remember, not my emergency."

He ended the tale by telling me not to take on other people's problems. I just looked at him for a few seconds and thought about what he said. This was brilliant! This man handled the situation with precision from the beginning and all the way to the ending. Throughout the entire time he stayed calm and didn't allow the other person to control the situation and stress him out over a problem that had nothing to do with him. I was very impressed by his attitude but I was more impressed by what I learned. Clearly he used his ability to Discern to determine that he would not get involved in a problem that was not his problem. Had he got involved, he would have placed himself and his family at a disadvantage. First, he would have been late picking up his son or he would have had to inconvenience someone else to get his son picked up. He then would have borrowed money from his mother, money his mother really didn't have to spare and money he really couldn't afford to pay her back. Furthermore, my co-worker had additional knowledge about this family member's track record of failing to pay back his debts because he already owes him money.

Utilizing all the information at his disposal, he said he would not put himself and his family in a negative position for someone who was clearly only thinking about his own needs and wants. I remember him saying to me, "How else would you characterize someone who asks to borrow money to keep the cable on and then requires you to bring the money to them? If that doesn't tell you all the information you need to know about this person, then I don't know what else to tell you."

Wow, another great morsel of information. I missed it the first go round. But once I thought about it, I realized my co-worker was right. It's one thing when someone asks you to assist with a problem they're having like borrowing money, it's another thing when they add on an additional problem for you, such as having you bring the money to them, especially since the situation is clearly not one of life and death. Only when you learn how to Discern will you take note of this information. Again, you don't take in the information solely to judge, even though a proper judgment must be made here; what you are really doing is taking in the information to assess whether or not you should get involved. Would it have made it difficult for my co-worker to bring this person the money and also pick up his son at the same time and cause a further chain reaction of unpleasant events for him? Absolutely! Therefore, based upon these facts, he determined that he would not get involved. This is classic Discernment in action. My co-worker methodically analyzed the information available to him and made a decision that was best for him and his family without feeling guilt, worry or stress. I couldn't stop thinking about how he handled everything from start to finish.

But here is the part that most people would have overlooked in this situation: my co-worker not getting involved did not place the family member in a worse situation. That determination has nothing to do with the fact that the family member found someone else to help him pay the cable. Even if the family member was unable to come up with the funds and the cable was turned off, my co-worker would not have been responsible for the problem spiraling downward. Why is that? It has to do with the fact that my co-worker did nothing to create the problem that was presented and he also did not have any obligation to provide assistance, especially if providing assistance meant taking away from his own immediate family. When someone analyzes available information to determine whether they will help another person in this type of situation, they need to sift through the information and also weigh the pros and cons of getting involved in a situation. If after sifting through the information, the person determines that providing help will tip the scale such that the helper is at a deficit, then they need not get involved. But more importantly, had the cable been turned off, it would not have been my co-worker's fault because it was not his problem to solve at any level. The problem simply existed when it came to my co-worker, so even if the problem got worse, my co-worker had no attachment to the problem from the onset and, therefore, the family member cannot assign blame to him at any stage or level of the problem.

You see, some people tend to assign blame to another person when that person decides not to help them with a problem. In their mind, if the problem gets worse, all of sudden the non-helper is to blame because they decided not to help. Well, I'm here to tell you: that's not how it works! It's your job as the one who Discerns properly to understand that your decision not to get involved includes not taking on the burden of guilt toward the person with the problem. Once you Discern your way through the situation, and Discernment dictates that you do not get involved, you've done your job; you must move on. Again, Discerning allows you to put the situation into perspective, make a healthy decision and move on without the burden of guilt or remorse because you know the decision was a correct one, just as it was with my co-worker. Focus on the objective parts of the situation and the path of what to do will become clear. My co-worker stayed focus on the pertinent facts and he came out on top. If you focus similarly, your outcome will be the same.

To assist you with assessing whether or not you should get involved in a situation such as this one, I've outlined an exercise/assessment test you should take that will keep you focused on the important facts that will lead you to determine whether or not your should get involved.

DISCERNING WHEN PRESENTED WITH AN 'EMERGENCY' - ASSESSMENT QUESTIONS

1. Is the problem a true 'emergency' where someone's life or liberty is at stake? If not, you should stop right here. When someone communicates to you that something is an 'emergency' and the situation is not a true 'emergency', this person is communicating so much to you about their character. You must pay attention.

2. Did the person position the problem as if the problem, somehow, is yours to solve?
3. Does the proposed solution as communicated to you add an additional obstacle for you to overcome in order to help?
4. Does getting involved cause you hardship or places you or your family somehow in a worse position by getting involved? If the answer is 'no' to any of these questions, then ask yourself what type of problem is it? Someone else's personal problem?
5. Does your involvement cause anyone else in your family any inconvenience or hardship?

As you can see, the answer to each question is important. One answer may give you a definitive answer that doesn't require any additional questions for you to consider. The answers that prompt additional questions will not confuse you. Rather, you will attain clarity that will help you truly understand the situation completely and not just one side of the story. In the end, you will have peace of mind because you will know what to do and you will be able to clearly articulate your position to the person without regret or feelings of remorse.

Situations where one has to *Discern* whether to lend money are situations that always provide the best lessons in *Discernment*. Let's look at another example where the crux of the matter is that someone is trying to place their problems in another person's lap.

Example 2: I Just Don't Have it to Give

Here is the dilemma that was presented to you: You have a favorite cousin you adore, a cousin who has helped you in the past by watching your children. You know that this cousin has a low-paying job and is a single mother of two boys and one girl. All of her children are under the age of 11. Today, she calls and asks you for money. You are not in a financial position to lend money to anyone, but you do know that your financial position is better than your cousin's financial position. Specifically, both you and your husband have good paying jobs but you also have four children of your own and one is in her first year of college. It is the beginning of Fall and all the kids are going back to school. You have just enough money for tuition, clothes and all the necessities for your children. You also have a sizable mortgage and made several repairs to the house over the summer that needed to be made. Basically, you are tapped out financially.

Your cousin is in need of money to purchase a used car. She is receiving child support from the children's father. She does have a job that pays a little more than minimum wage, but she does not have enough money to purchase a car that costs $2,500.00. She has come to you for the full $2,500.00. She promises that she will pay you back in three weeks but you recall that she borrowed $1,000.00 from you three years ago and you are still waiting to receive payment. This family member is a great person, one of your favorites, but you simply do not have the money to lend and if you did decide to lend out money, you would definitely need the money back within the three weeks in order to fulfill certain needs for your family. So now the question is: considering all of this information, will you lend your cousin the money or not?

Once again, all the information you need in order to make the right decision is available to you. Using your ability to Discern, you should confidently conclude that you should not lend the family member the money. Why? First and foremost, you already know that you do not have the money to lend. End of story! All of the other factors and pieces of information just serve to create confusion and will provoke you to act on emotion. What is the biggest distractor in this scenario? It is the fact that you love and care for this person. You need to understand that if you love someone, you will still love them even though you may not be in a financial position to help them. If you are caught up on the love and affection you feel for this person, and you feel the need to get involved, then you can help them figure out a way of solving the problem without it hurting you. This is not easy, but you must navigate your way through this situation rationally. Using your ability to Discern in this situation will make sure you do just that.

For example, perhaps you can suggest that your cousin consider buying a car that costs less money. Maybe you can help her construct a budget that will assist her in working towards purchasing a car that she can afford. Even further, maybe after you look at your own budget, you may determine that you can help her out with some money next month or a couple of months down the road. The possibilities are plentiful, but you must look at the situation fully and objectively in order to Discern what you can or cannot do.

This is especially true if the person truly matters to you. No one is saying you have to ignore your feelings completely; that's not realistic. But you absolutely must put your feelings in check and focus on the facts in order to grasp that win-win scenario that is within your reach. There is nothing worse than helping someone you love in a way that places you at a disadvantage. This type of help often backfires on you. Bad blood can be created when you help someone in a situation where the person could have waited or the person should have used a more appropriate alternative to solving their problem. But instead you allowed them to deprive you of something that you needed for you and your family. Do you know what this may lead to? Feelings of regret, anger and a host of other emotions. If you Discern the situation <u>after the fact</u>, you will find that the more you lament on what you did, you may begin resenting the person you helped. This is exactly why Discernment needs to take place upfront, not on the back end. The back end leaves you with remorse, regret, hurt and anger. In other words, the back end leaves you with even more emotions than you started with. Discern in the beginning to avoid this trap because you do not need any additional emotions to grapple with. If you succumb to this trap, you run the high risk of harboring resentment towards someone you love and care about when you finally realize that you put them first to the detriment of yourself and your immediate family. This is not just about saying No. More importantly, it's about choosing the right outcome for the right reasons.

If nothing else, when you Discern, you are sifting through all types of information—good, bad, irrelevant and crucial—before you can be routed to the correct decision. Depending upon how well you have developed your ability to Discern, you may need to sift through all the information before making a decision. But let me share with you that someone who Discerns regularly and consistently, however, would have determined on the spot that the answer in this scenario was 'no' because they do not have the money to give. The fact that this family member already owes you money and hasn't paid it back as promised is also relevant information in deciding whether to lend this person money, especially if you need the money back within a certain timeframe. Since you already know this person does not pay back on time and you need the money back in order to fulfill your own obligations, why would you lend to someone who you already know you can't rely upon to pay you back in time? In the words of Tina Turner, "what's love got to do with it?" You are setting yourself up for failure by placing yourself at the mercy of someone who you know is not reliable. Please do not do this to yourself and your family.

There's lots of relevant information in this situation that will help you make the right decision, but really the primary information you needed to pinpoint is the fact that you are not in a financial position to lend out that money. This is a fact. If you ignored that fact and was leaning towards lending your cousin money due to your affection for her, the second piece of information about her payment history should have been the next gate-keeper to stop you. That information is the fact that this person already owes you money that she has not paid back for three years. You also know that you need this money for your own children, therefore you have no business placing yourself in a position that will have an adverse effect on your family. Again, the only way you would lend the money under these circumstances is to allow anything other than the facts take over your decision-making. In other words, you would toss your ability to Discern to the side and act on your affinity for this family member who has helped you out in the past. As admirable and heartfelt as this sounds, it is not a good idea.

Using your ability to Discern will never allow you to place your family in a negative position in order to benefit someone else. The fact is that you are not responsible for the position this family member has found herself in and you are not responsible for improving her condition at your expense. Under the current facts, you simply cannot help her and, quite frankly, there are other options that may be available to her that she should pursue. This is not your problem to solve if it will cause you and your family to suffer in any way. But if you insist on helping her, you need to do so cautiously and responsibly. Here is an assessment test to use in this situation.

DISCERNING WHEN LENDING MONEY - ASSESSMENT QUESTIONS

1. Are you in a financial position to lend out money? If the answer is 'no' you need not go any further with an analysis. You need to inform the person that you are unable to assist at this time.
2. If you determine that you cannot assist at the present time but

you can assist in the future, you will need to assess if the future assistance is feasible and will not leave you at a deficit. Some of the questions will require you to focus on the person borrowing the money.
3. Will you need the money back within a time certain? If so, how reliable is the borrower?
4. If the person is reliable, then you can proceed with lending what you can afford. If you are unsure if the person is reliable, you should either decide not to lend the money or inquire as much as you can to determine if you should lend the money.
5. Before lending the money, make sure lending the money will not cause problems between you and your family. If it will, do not lend.

GUIDELINES FOR LENDING MONEY

An extra step in making appropriate assessments with lending money is establishing rules for lending money. Establishing rules with money lending aids tremendously in the *Discernment Process* because it provides a firm basis or condition upon which you are able to lend money.

Personally, I have a firm rule for lending money to anyone. Here is my rule: If I have the money to give without needing it back or without having to ask for the money back, then I will lend the money. However, if I am not able to give out money without needing it back, I will not lend it out. This rule takes the financial burden aspect off me.

I also only lend to those who I believe would pay me back without me having to ask for it. This, as you know, requires me to *Discern* certain pertinent information about this person's character, especially since this is personal. Therefore, I need to set these rules and then make sure the person I'm potentially lending to fits the criteria set forth in the rules. This analysis is no different than what a financial institution does when lending money. And if you are lending money professionally, seek the advice of an attorney.

Let's now look at a third example of a situation where *Discerning* identifies a situation that may sound appealing to you but will end up as a win-win for one person but a lose-lose scenario for another.

Example 3: You win, I lose!

No one is immune from unappealing situations that come their way, even me. When I was about 23 years old, I was studying law abroad in London, England and met a musician one day as I was crossing a street. I was out with some friends at the time. My eyes met the musician as we were both crossing the street in the opposite direction. Once I almost finished crossing the street, I looked back to see where he was and noticed that he stopped in the middle of the street and was staring at me. I smiled at him, turned my head and continued walking with my friends hoping that he would come up to me. I had already decided that I could not speak to him first because that's just how I was raised. I felt that he should be the one to come up to me first. Luckily, he crossed the street again, came up to me and said "Hi." Still walking, slowly, I said "Hello" and then he quickly asked if I liked jazz music. I told him that I loved jazz and he said "great." By this time we were on the sidewalk and we stopped to talk. He told me he was playing at a club that night and if I were interested, please come, with my friends, as his guests. I was instructed to tell the person at the door that "the saxophone player sent me." He never told me his name. He smiled and then hurried along his way; I excitedly turned to my friends and asked them to join me that night and they said "yes."

After getting myself ready for the rest of the day, my friends and I anxiously headed out to attend the show at the famous jazz club in Soho, London known as Ronnie Scotts. At the time, I didn't know that so many of the jazz giants played at this cozy club. Anyway, we met the band afterwards. After the show, the musician and I grabbed a bite to eat, without my friends, and began dating shortly thereafter. We both were from the U.S. so it wouldn't be such a big deal seeing each other after we both left the U.K. We spent time experiencing London for a couple of months and then perhaps on our ninth or tenth wonderful date, he informed me that he was leaving London and would be traveling across the U.S. and other countries for approximately six months. He said he'd love to continue seeing me and would pay for all of my travel whenever we'd see each other. And just when I didn't think this story could get any better, he said to me in such a calm, sweet voice, "But I just want you to know that I am not in a position to be faithful to anyone. My life is spent traveling all over so I do not believe in long distance relationships. But whenever I'm close by or close enough for me to send for you, I will. And that's the best I can do right now."

Hearing this I think my heart skipped a few beats. To be honest, I was truly caught off guard. If you asked me five seconds before this happened, I would have told you he was the one. I didn't see this coming at all. So now, in light of all the fun I was having abroad, how was I supposed to process this information? I must have had a look of total shock when he spoke these words to me. I'm not sure what my first initial response was, but what I can tell you definitively is that, with those four sentences, he provided me with all the information I needed to make the proper decision at that time. There were only three ways I could have responded to the information and proposal he presented to me:

1. I could accept his proposal and become one of the women he sees when it suits him,
2. I could reject what he said and try to convince him to date only me, or
3. I could respectfully decline the offer and move on with my life.

So let me give you some additional information about me that plays a significant role in how I processed the information given to me: 1. My personality/character, 2. My life experiences, and 3. My Emotional IQ. My personality is more on the quiet introverted side. I keep my feelings to myself. For the most part, in matters of the heart, I keep my feelings of love to myself unless I feel safe to do otherwise. Nine times out of ten, I would determine it unwise to divulge my feelings to anyone. In other words, I am good at not showing my emotions. My sister would always say to me, "never let 'em see you sweat!" She was referring to not allowing anyone see that they hurt or angered me, particularly when I did nothing to hurt or anger the person. This positioning is perhaps the best way to describe me. In my mind, if I made a determination that you hurt me unnecessarily, all emotions are shut off and I proceed on what I believe to be the only logical course of action. Understand that such a disposition leads to decision-making based upon more factual information and takes you out of the arena of being hurt.

Now understand that if I am *Discerning* in this situation, there is really only one option to choose under these circumstances. *Discerning* dictates that I choose option #3. Here is why option #3 was the only rational decision for me at the time.

THE MAYA ANGELOU PRINCIPLE

One of my favorite quotes in the world and one of the mantras I live by is a quote by the Beloved Maya Angelou who once said, "When people show you who they are, believe them the first time."

I could write a dissertation on this quote alone because there is so much information packed into that one phrase. If you truly understood what Ms. Angelou was saying, you'd know that her words were really all about *Discernment*. Put in different words, she really said: 'when a person provides you with direct information about who they are, believe what they told you the first time they told you.' So often people tell us things about themselves, information which tells us emphatically to either leave them alone or proceed with extreme caution for a limited purpose—while keeping in mind that information they provided to you—and we just don't want to believe them or we allow other distractors to cloud our judgment towards that person. We do this, despite being given specific information about the person that came right from the person's mouth.

Once we make the decision to ignore the information that was handed to us on a silver platter, we set ourselves up for failure and, in some instances, we set ourselves up for danger. Take this example that I just gave you about my love interest. First, you must *Discern* that, not only are options 1 and 2 in the musician's best interests, but they are options that may very well end up hurting me in more ways than one. If I allowed myself to be distracted, I would say to myself, 'this man was bold and honest enough to tell me that he would not be in a monogamous relationship with me. Therefore, he's not a bad guy. I should continue this relationship. I can convince him to date only me; I can change him.' So many women truly believe they can change a man even though such a change is truly beyond their control. In addition, I can even admire the fact that he was upfront with the information. But here's the true big ticket item of information that I need to be even more impressed with: he was essentially telling me that he wanted a relationship that would put his needs first, not mine and not ours; he was telling me that his goal was to benefit himself, not me and not us. In fact, there is no US here. He clearly wanted a relationship on his terms even though his terms would be hurtful to me. In fact, his words communicated to me that there is no 'us', only 'me'. The fact that he said it nicely and was upfront about his motives were irrelevant pieces of information that I didn't need to focus on. The most important information he gave was the fact that he was putting himself first. And guess what? I believe exactly what he told me without any further information. I also believe he was hoping I was distracted by the handsome package in which he presented the information and he was further hoping that I was distracted by the wonderful time I had with him over the past two months so as to ignore what he was truly saying.

And if I were acting upon my feelings, selfishness, temporary gratification and a whole host of other distractions, other than the direct information that was presented to me, I would have been distracted to the point of placing myself in an unwanted position that may have lead to a number of issues further down the road.

In a nutshell, I could have potentially exposed myself to physical and emotional issues by continuing this relationship. This is why if you are confronted with a proposition such as this, you must focus on the information you have and not lead with distractors. Distractors are just that; things that distract you from the facts and will cause you to make choices that are not in your best interests.

Another important point, and actually the main point, to always keep in mind about *Discernment* is this: your decisions will NOT leave YOU in the lurch. The whole point of *Discerning* is to make decisions that will positively impact your life. People with big, soft hearts tend to forego this point to their detriment. Individuals with big hearts tend to make decisions to help others that only serve to hurt them in the end. *Discernment* doesn't allow this to happen. So in this situation, as I used my ability to *Discern*, it became clear to me that I needed to walk away from this relationship and that's exactly what I did. And you know what else? If this relationship was truly meant to be, then I believe we would have found ourselves back to each other; there is no need for me to force anything. After you *Discern*, you can look at future outcomes with a person more objectively and realistically. This is how I was able to come to the conclusion that the future can take care of itself. True love is not something that needs to be forced upon anyone. On the other hand, if I acted on my emotions and falsely believed that I must act on what he proposed or else I would lose him, I would have missed the fact that I never had him to begin with. This fact is a very sobering fact; one that most people couldn't admit to themselves. You have to really humble yourself in order to swallow that bitter pill. But I did it, almost instantly. Sure, it hurt. But it's better to hurt a little now then to hurt a whole lot more on the back end. I have no doubt that if I accepted what was presented to me, I would have acted out of fear… fear of losing these past two months. But the truth is, the past two months will never be taken away. What can be taken away from me, however, is my dignity, my self-worth, my ability to trust and perhaps a lot more. Learning to *Discern* in the face of this type of situation is the way to go.

These are just a few examples of how using your ability to *Discern* will keep you and/or your loved ones from suffering unnecessarily. In all three situations, deciding not to get involved or deciding to bow out gracefully was the right course of action because the information provided was just enough to know that getting involved would hurt you and yours more than it would help the other person in need. And knowing what we now know about *Discernment*, we are clear that *Discernment* does NOT set you up for hurt or suffering.

More often than not, people ignore the fact that their disposition does not allow for them to get involved in certain situations. Instead of realizing this fact, people are more focused on assessing other people's situation FIRST to see how bad the person's situation is; subconsciously, they do this with the goal of determining whether someone else's situation is worse than their own situation. For some, this assessment provides a type of enjoyment and then a basis to help the other person. Clearly this type of help is misplaced and ill-conceived. Help should never be given to another on the premise that one is somehow superior to another. Feeling better about oneself by assessing the misfortunes of another is a form of self-loathing. Anytime someone feels a sense of gratification based upon the unfortunate circumstances of another, it's because their life is not fulfilling either. They have not found their purpose; they may even be hurting in some way. As imperfect humans who each have their own problems and issues to deal with, many of us are inclined to make such an assessment of others because we have not examined our own lives enough or perhaps at all. It may be true that someone's situation is worse than yours; however, just because someone else's current status is worse than yours, doesn't mean your situation is a good one. It also doesn't mean your situation will eventually improve nor does it mean your situation cannot become worse than the other person's at some point. And, to be blunt about it, if we are trying to be our best self and be accountable for the choices we make in life, we wouldn't need to assess anyone else's shortcomings and compare them to our own anyway. Instead, if we took the time to focus on improving our own situation rather than making ourselves feel better through someone else's misfortunes, we'd realize that we simply cannot afford to help that person even though we have the mindset to do so. If you really want to help someone in need, help yourself first so that you can be in a position to help someone else. Another way to bring this point home is to think about what happens on an airplane.

Have you ever thought about the fact that every time you board an airplane, at the beginning of every flight, the flight attendants go over the safety features of the aircraft and demonstrate what to do in case of an emergency. When the attendant discusses the possibility of passengers needing oxygen due to a change in cabin pressure, they tell you that oxygen masks will be released. They also inform you that once the mask is placed over the face properly, oxygen will freely flow from the mask. But the salient piece of information that the attendant tells you is this: **if someone else needs assistance with their oxygen mask, you must FIRST place the oxygen mask over yourself and then proceed**

to help another person with their oxygen mask. The attendant does not make any allowances or exceptions for certain people who may need assistance with oxygen. The rule is straightforward: place the oxygen mask on yourself FIRST before you help anyone else with their oxygen mask!

Let's first recognize that this is a rule put in place uniformly by all airlines for the safety and protection of everyone aboard the aircraft. Now, the reason for this rule is simple: you cannot help someone else who is suffering when you're suffering. Put another way, you cannot help someone out of a negative situation when you are operating from a negative position. This is a fact. As awful as this may sound, even lifeguards are trained to know when to let someone drown. I'm sorry to say this, but it's true. If the lifeguard is presented with a situation where he cannot save a stranger without drowning both himself and the stranger, what is he expected to do? The answer is obvious; he would be expected to save himself, unless, perhaps, a child was involved.

Now, with respect to the oxygen masks on an aircraft, the pertinent information about the oxygen masks is spoken at the beginning of each and every flight. Yet and still, I'm sure there are some individuals who, if faced with a situation where the oxygen masks are released, would reach for the oxygen mask for their loved ones first, especially their young children, before placing the mask over their face first. Why? Because as perfectly-flawed human beings, that's our first response and it is also the emotional response. It is natural for any parent to attempt to place an oxygen mask over their child first before thinking of themselves. However, *Discernment* makes us aware that leading with our emotions begets poor decision-making, especially when the correct information is staring you in the face. It may seem to you that helping the child with their mask first is the right thing to do, however, that's not the case and the flight attendant already told you so outright. Therefore, you attempting to place the mask on your loved ones first is you NOT using your ability to *Discern*. Instead, it is you allowing your emotions to dictate your actions. You must comprehend that using your ability to *Discern* will ensure that you avoid this pitfall. By going against the flight attendant's specific instructions, you are placing yourself and anyone you are helping with an oxygen mask in more danger than initially exists. I'm quite sure this would not be your intended outcome as you are reaching for the oxygen mask. So the lesson is: ignoring information that is available to you is you NOT utilizing your ability to *Discern*. Continuing to act in this manner will cause you to make unnecessary mistakes, some of which may be fatal.

I believe you now have enough examples and strategies in this chapter to absorb and reflect upon. Now let's continue discussing what *Discernment* is NOT.

Discernment is not about winning an argument; and it is certainly not about a definitive determination of 'right' and 'wrong'. Even deeper, *Discernment* is not about a concrete determination of 'truth' and 'error'. *Discernment* is much more fluid and uplifting than that; *Discernment* can be found on a much higher level of thinking than merely being 'right' or 'wrong', 'black or white'. If your goal in making decisions in life is to confirm that you are right, you are definitely not *Discerning*. In fact, you do not completely understand what *Discernment* is if all you want to be is 'right'. The whole notion of engaging someone or making decisions in life just to prove that you are right is not only a low-level of thinking, it is outright dangerous. People who operate in that manner win battles but always lose wars. That's because they refuse to grasp the broader concept of what it means to operate from a position of humility. Instead, they are operating from a totally different angle filled with emotional markers. And if they are obsessed with being crowned 'right' and someone else being dubbed 'wrong', they are a slave to pride. Pride is, arguably, the most destructive element that someone can lead with during their decision-making. Pride and its qualities will be discussed in Chapter Six.

Individuals who seek to always prove they are right are merely surviving in life. Living in survival mode presents a breeding ground for irrational and poor thinking. If you are operating in survival mode, your ability to *Discern* becomes overshadowed or muted by emotions, preconceived notions, prejudices and selfish desires that will dictate a person's responses and reactions. Most of these bad habits and beliefs are learned behaviors and we, as creatures of habit, refuse to let go of such destructive patterns and thought processes. By holding onto these shortcomings, one will never truly develop an ability to *Discern*; instead such persons cling onto a mindset that is destructive. However, if you let go of these falsehoods, being able to *Discern* now becomes a possibility along with the opportunity to take control of your life by engaging in self-reflection and tapping into your God-given internal guidance and reasoning skills as various situations arise. And the good news is that when you learn how to *Discern* in the small situations, you are also preparing yourself how to *Discern* in the larger more intense situations where a lot more is at stake.

And last but certainly not least, *Discernment* is NOT meant to be a quick fix or a temporary solution to a problem. Quite the opposite, *Discernment* takes into consideration the relevant factors to ensure that the choices you make will not cause you to back track, back peddle or reverse course. More importantly, *Discernment* is forward-moving, forward-looking and forward-thinking. In other words, *Discernment* focuses on the bigger picture which takes into account your future and not just what is happening today. Temporary self-gratification is not the end result of the *Discernment* Process. If *Discernment* is involved in the course of action you chose, you will feel confident that the right decision was made right now and for the future. Start with the assessment questions provided in this chapter to help increase your understanding of *Discernment* and to assist with the development of your ability to *Discern*. What you will learn is that the more you *Discern*, the better you will become at knowing what *Discernment* is and what *Discernment* IS NOT.

Chapter Five

DISCERNMENT, CORE VALUES, PRINCIPLES & RULES

The reality of life is that we all have certain characteristics, habits, mannerisms, prejudices and opinions that we carry around with us on a daily basis. That's why whenever someone says to me, 'I'm not prejudice' or 'I don't discriminate against anyone,' it always give me cause to pause for a second or two. Hearing those words, I have to decide whether I'm going to respond to the statement or simply acknowledge it and let the topic go. My chosen response or lack thereof is one of *Discernment* because I will need to make a judgment call on what to do with such information. And clearly my decision will be based upon the particular person I'm conversing with as well as the context of the conversation. But know this: no matter the person, context or why the statement was made, the person making the statement is really conveying to me part of their belief system or Core Values.

What are Core Values? Core Values make up the belief system and guiding principles you live by. You probably already have certain values or principles and beliefs you live by without actually calling them 'Core Values'. These principles and beliefs are what shape your behavior and thought process; they also guide the decisions you make in life. Having Core Values is an essential framework that should be used as a backdrop for *Discernment*. Why? Because if you stand on certain principles, you will have a sound basis upon which to make decisions that are appropriate for you and yours. But please understand that Core Values, just like any of our personal beliefs, can be used to justify our wrongdoing when we haven't taken the time to analyze why we have such beliefs and how we actually use them on a daily basis; this is why self-reflection in life is key. It is up to you to make a conscious effort to take an inventory of what your current beliefs are, where they came from and what, if any, changes to this belief system you need to make.

Now getting back to the statements 'I'm not prejudice' or 'I don't discriminate against anyone', they are wonderful beliefs but both statements are downright hard to believe. Often times when we think of prejudice and discrimination, we think in terms of race, color, gender or sexual orientation. But quite frankly, the ways in which we constantly discriminate against individuals are done so in ways not necessarily connected to race, color, gender or sexual orientation; many times we don't even realize we're discriminating against someone, but we are. Or better yet, we justify our discriminatory behavior and pat ourselves on the back for our ingenuity in masking our actions as anything but discrimination or prejudice. There are several categories of people that come to mind on the topic of discrimination: age, employment status, social status, familial status and physical appearance. We may act out our prejudice by moving our seat, refusing to acknowledge someone or walking in the opposite direction of someone who we don't know and have determined we don't want to know on the basis of their size or appearance. When we make such decisions to move or somehow indicate our disdain for someone based upon these shallow reasons, rest assured that your decisions are rooted in prejudice, not *Discernment*. Nothing in those types of decisions or judgments seek to elevate or uplift anyone, including yourself. The only purpose is to condemn, judge or separate. And although our actions may not be punishable by law, that does not mean the behavior was not discriminatory in nature. But alas, if you dared to think about what you did and why you did it, it is!

I'm not saying that we can't aspire to be less prejudice or limit our prejudice to rational judgment calls that serve to protect us rather than to hurt or judge others, because that is exactly what we should do. But in order to do that, we must be honest with ourselves and face the fact that none of us are blameless in our walk of life. At some point or another, we all have passed judgment or discriminated against someone and somehow justified our decision to ourselves or to anyone who we trust enough to listen. And the fact of the matter is, this is a learned behavior. Suffice it to say, it took a long time for us to accumulate this type of baggage we carry around with us; and it's safe to say that it takes awhile for us to undo all the damage done from carrying such baggage; our constant rush to judgment is, indeed, invisible baggage that weighs us down in countless ways. And since we probably started carrying this baggage from an early age, we are immune to how heavy it has become over the years.

Let's face it, making changes in life is difficult. Making changes requires discipline, determination and persistence in order for us to see the necessary changes actually come to fruition. This is why learning to *Discern* in the face of establishing Core Values and using them consciously will help you make the changes you need to make. Learning to *Discern* properly also requires a level of discipline in order for you to consistently make appropriate decisions. You will have to fight multiple urges, old habits, emotions and so many elements that are designed to keep you off track. Therefore, because you will be fighting several battlefronts, you should start with a foundation or strategy you can use before, during and after you are confronted with all types of situations. If you have a strategy, it will set the stage for you to begin *Discerning* as you make important decisions. A great place to start is by establishing Core Values. The bottom line is, it's time for you to develop your own belief system instead of living on a belief system that was fed to you. It's time to build your own solid foundation of Core Values.

The list of Core Values is plentiful. You can find hundreds of Core Values on the internet or in books devoted to professional development. On a professional level, many organizations define their Core

Values and use them to constantly evaluate their mission effectiveness. On a personal level, your parents probably had a set of Core Values they learned from their parents and then passed them down to you during your upbringing. As life goes on and we become adults, we tend to hang onto the Core Values we were exposed to at home, in school, from friends, through secondary education, through our religious beliefs and perhaps through various life experiences. We then incorporate these Core Values into our adult lives at home, at work, with friends, family and any relationships we form. We generally hold onto these values seamlessly as we age without seriously questioning ourselves as to how we got here. Whether or not we stick to these inherited Core Values depends on the person; if we do stick to them, the consistency in which we adhere to them depends upon the nature of each of the relationships we form and develop throughout life. For example, falling in love tends to be a situation where not only will we dispense with some of our Core Values in the moment, but we may even let a Core Value or two go for good as the love grows stronger. Depending upon who you're in love with, this may be a good or a bad thing. However, if you never take the time to understand what your values are and why you believe in them, you may be throwing away certain Core Values at a time when you need them the most. Therefore, knowing what you truly stand for and why you've taken such a stand will stop you from tossing your principles and values aside when you really need them to guide you through important situations.

Since for most of us the Core Values we're following were not established by way of a list we sat down to compile ourselves, it's high time that we actually sit down and create a list of Core Values we stand by and are committed to upholding. To help you with developing an appropriate list of Core Values for yourself, this book lists 50 of the most widely used Core Values. I then identify 10 Core Values that many of us have in common. From the list of 10 commonly shared Core Values, I highlight 5 Core Values to discuss in detail. Finally, I discuss 2 crucial Core Values that I believe everyone should uphold. At the conclusion of these discussions, I strike at the heart of why certain Core Values are so important to the topic of *Discernment*.

50 Most Widely Used Core Values

Family	Commitment	Determination	Purpose	Tolerance
Integrity	Understanding	Gratitude	Responsibility	Sincerity
Fairness	Honesty	Growth	Selfless	Motivation
Justice	Accountability	Happiness	Service	Honor
Love	Trust	Humility	Giving	Equality
Loyalty	Adaptability	Hope	Thankful	Discipline
Respect	Ambition	Integrity	Success	Community
Spiritual	Consistency	Kindness	Wealth	Dignity
Peace	Justice	Maturity	Wisdom	Health
Truth	Courage	Persistence	Tradition	Compassion

10 Commonly Shared Core Values

Family	Truth	Respect	Love	Happiness
Loyalty	Trust	Wisdom	Success	Compassion

Top 5 Core Values

Family   Love   Respect   Happiness   Success

1 - CORE VALUE - FAMILY

The first Core Value I chose to lead with is the Core Value of 'Family'. I choose to discuss Family first because Family is the first Core Value we are exposed to and the one that has the biggest effect upon our lives. Whether you're born into a family steeped in rich traditions, or you've just reached the age of 45 and are still searching for the birth parents who gave you away or even if you grew up in foster care, that initial family environment we are raised in shapes the lens through which we see the world. The family structure you're born and raised in is the environment that sets the foundation for your belief system. Your concept of family and how important you view family will determine so much in your life. This book cannot possibly discuss all the varied dynamics and sorted factors found in different family structures around the world because the variations are countless. But we will explore the ways in which family can serve to uplift or hinder your progress depending upon how YOU interpret family and how you allow family to function in your life.

Whenever I begin a discussion about family and the role it plays in one's life, no matter what the context, I always give my audience a disclaimer. That is, I always state the following:

> *'My concept of family may not be the norm and may even be considered 'warped' by some standards. I am not here to diminish the level of importance family plays in your life; I am just trying to understand how you view family and what role that view plays in your life currently. Once you understand your family dynamic, your personal view of family and how that dynamic and view of family affects the decisions you make in life, you will begin to pay closer attention to how family has and continues to impact you, your goals and your path in life. It is only when you understand this impact that you will decide what changes and boundaries you must implement with certain family members. Sometimes the boundaries will need to be established in order to ensure that you're not led astray for the sake of family. Overall, you need to understand how you have interpreted family in the past and how you will interpret family going forward.'*

Those statements tend to peak my audience's interest because now they really want to know how my view of family may be 'warped' and how family can lead someone astray. As the discussion progresses, they begin to think about family relationships in their lives and, perhaps, begin truly reflecting on these relationships for the very first time.

For me, I learned at an early age how to define and view family in a way that would not limit me or somehow overshadow or interfere with my dreams. Now some people hearing this information will wonder how can family get in the way of your dreams. My answer has been and will always be the same: *family, or anyone for that matter, can only hinder your life or your progress in life if you allow them to do so.* Just like friends, co-workers and significant others, family members come with their own set of problems and issues that show up when they come to you. The major difference between family and anyone else you interact with in life is the fact that you don't have the luxury of choosing the family you are born into or those you are related to by blood or even those who married into your family. Unfortunately, this difference is often the way family can act as a stronghold to your detriment. If you fail to recognize when certain family members use the high value you place on family as a way to benefit themselves at your expense, you are headed for major setbacks without even knowing it. This tends to happen to people who believe that 'nothing is more important than family.' A person who wholeheartedly believes in this statement and is dedicated to family without conditions or boundaries will always place family ahead of their own needs no matter what the situation. Such persons generally suffer in silence and feel a sense of selflessness because they sacrifice for the sake of family.

Understand that there is nothing wrong with making sacrifices for your family at various times in life. In fact, most of us do it, especially for our children, spouses, parents and other family members in our lives who we love. However, when these sacrifices are made in the absence of *Discernment*, the disposition can and often times leave you vulnerable to being taken advantage of consistently. Nice, big-hearted people are the victims of this scam perpetrated by selfish family members. Such family members will seize upon your sentimental attachment to family and your unyielding duty to assist family members in need at all times. The result may be that you are constantly placing others' needs before your own to the point that you will not fulfill your goals. If this continues to happen, eventually you will harbor resentment and bitterness that will eat away at you until you either finally say 'no' to family members, sever the familial relationship or until the family member betrays you in a way you didn't see coming due to your limitless obligation to family. If that happens, you will have to come to terms with the fact that you created this exhaustive obligation that has been exploited for years with your express consent. If you allow family to function this way in your life, the manner in which you've handled family will catch up to you eventually and the end result will not be pretty.

Establishing Boundaries from a Position of *Discernment*

The first order of business is to be acutely aware of how you perceive certain things in life. For example, some people consider the word 'boundaries' to be a negative word. They may interpret this word in such a way that they question whether they need boundaries in the first place. For example, some people see boundaries as restrictions, conditions, limits or barriers. You should realize that placing things in a negative light gives you a reason not to consider implementing important changes at all. Instead, I like to look at boundaries as protectors or safeguards. I say this because the true purpose of boundaries is to protect you and those around you from harm. Personal boundaries are not necessarily meant to scare people away but if it does, 9 times out of 10 it scares the people you need to protect yourself from anyway. Such an unintended result is an appropriate by-product of establishing boundaries that works in your favor. This is why you shouldn't be afraid to set up boundaries in your life. Moreover, in many instances, boundaries actually protect the person or persons whom you are enforcing the boundaries against also, but more than likely they will not see it that way. They will only see the boundaries you created against them in the negative because they're not thinking about it the way you are. They are in 'circumstance mode'; they are not *Discerning*, you are. They will not understand that your boundaries are all-around protectors for all concerned. Therefore, it's up to you to stay focused and continue with the boundaries in order to stay protected. Boundaries should be implemented with good intentions. Intentions are paramount. Keeping your head in the game at all times will ensure that you will do the right thing when establishing boundaries. When I say keep your head in the game, understand that I'm talking about establishing your boundaries from a position of *Discernment*, of course.

Here is another important point you should know about setting boundaries. **Ideally, boundaries should be implemented before you have a problem with someone**. You do not wait until someone abuses your friendship, kindness or generosity and then you pull back from the person ... even though this is usually how we operate. This is how relationships become fractured and sometimes destructive; that's not what you want. Setting boundaries for yourself before relationships begin help you *Discern* early on whether this is a relationship you should even initiate. You need to start taking stock in the type of person you are, what type of people you allow in your life and be conscious of how these people treat you. Let's look at an example of a scenario where you should implement boundaries:

BFFs

Let's say you have 3 core friends you hang around with in and out of school; you all went to high school together and you consider them to be your best friends. You are all going to local colleges and you are all in your second year of college. Your are often teased by your friends and other schoolmates that you are the nice one of the group. This month you turned 19 and you are the last one in the group to turn 19. When each of your friends turned 19, their parents bought a used car for them to have access to. They are allowed to use the car periodically to go out with friends, go to school, and run errands for the house whenever they are home. Whenever you go out with your friends, instead of riding in your friends' cars, your parents make it a point to drive you to the destination and pick you up most of the time. During the few times your parents allowed you to ride in your friends' vehicles, they insisted upon you giving your friends gas money. But again, your parents do not allow you to ride in your friends' vehicles often. On the other hand, none of your other friends reciprocated when they rode in any of the other friends' cars.

Now that you turned 19, your parents decided that part of your birthday gift would be to give you access to a car as well. However, instead of a used car, your parents have given you access to a brand new car they purchased as the new family car. Now that means you and your friends all have access to a car. Your parents thought about buying you a used car just like your friends' parents but since your parents know and appreciate your responsible behavior, they decided to give you access to the brand new car instead. They and everyone else know that you are a trustworthy person.

All of your friends love the new car and love riding in it even more than their cars. As you all continue to meet up at the mall, college events and other social outings, you notice that your friends now always expect you to drive, pick them up, and drop them off at their homes or college dorm. Their rationale, of course, is the fact that you have the nicest car of all of them and they all look so much more attractive when they all show up in your car. The other parents don't seem to mind this disposition. However, despite you always providing gas money whenever you rode in anyone else's car, not one of your friends or their parents even offers gas money to you whenever the four of you ride together in your new car.

You have not informed your parents of what is going on but you are starting to get concerned that you are placing a lot of miles on the car (which your parents warned you about) and you are using a significant amount of your allowance to pay for gas. Because you are responsible, up until now you never had a problem with your allowance. But you know if you continue on this route, you will have to ask your parents for an increase and explain why it's necessary. You want to say something to your friends but you don't want to hurt anyone's feelings or damage any of your friendships. After all, they are your BFFs. But as the days go by, you realize that something has to change. What should you do? Should you establish boundaries under these circumstances?

The answer is yes, immediately, and without question. The question here is: How are you going to implement boundaries?

Assess the Situation

In looking at the facts, you can see how this situation spiraled out of control. Here are some pertinent facts that should have alerted you to the fact that boundaries were in order:

Facts about you:

1. 'You are the nice one in the group'
2. 'You are responsible'
3. You always offered gas when you rode in someone else's car.

Facts about your friends:

1. They all ride in your car consistently without offering gas money even though you always gave them gas money and they accepted the money.
2. They all allowed you to suffer financially as the driver without sharing the burden, knowing that you shared that financial burden as it applied to their cars.

A notation should also be made about the parents, especially the fact that your parents were considerate of your friends by making sure you provided gas money to them. However, your friends' parents did not do the same. Honestly, as a parent I would have *Discerned* that I will limit and watch closely my child's friendship with these individuals because it is clear that their parents don't exactly have the same Core Values or ethical standards as me. I would educate my child on the facts. Again, the intent is to not hurt anyone, but I would give my child the facts so that he could see what is going on here.

Getting back to the students, this goes back to what I said earlier. You should have been able to avoid this situation by doing the following: *taking stock in the type of person you are, what type of people you allow in your life and be conscious of how these people treat you.* Even if you didn't know it before, you can see how your kindness was exploited by your friends. Some people tend to exploit kindness at any opportunity. It is your job to protect yourself and not allow people to change you from being you. Any changes you make should be made on your terms. The way you do this is by setting boundaries.

In the scenario I gave you, even if your friends didn't intend to exploit your kindness, the fact is, they did. If you continue to allow them to do this, you will pay a huge price for it. You must now place boundaries on their use of your parents' car. How do you do this? Start with the following:

1. Tell them you should all take turns driving their cars when they meet up.

2. Tell them that everyone should pitch in gas money to whoever is driving. Also tell them that the amount of the contribution toward gas money depends upon the distance you must travel to the destination.

These boundaries will protect all involved and it promotes equality and shared financial responsibility. If your friends fail to respect these boundaries, you will need to make additional changes to the relationships as needed. In some cases you may need to sever relationships. This is classic *Discernment* in action. I do not believe you need to explain boundaries to anyone. However, if you decide to explain why these boundaries are being implemented, you can explain to your friends why these boundaries are necessary. Once the boundaries are implemented, you will discover who are your real friends and who are not. In other words, you will see who respects the boundaries and who will not. Now let's get back to people who are relentlessly committed to the Core Value of Family.

People who place a limitless value on family would be surprised to hear that family should be managed from a position of *Discernment*. The fact is, all relationships should be navigated with *Discernment* in mind, especially family and intimate relationships since they are the ones that have the potential to hurt you in some of the most severe ways. Once again, the way to navigate these crucial relationships, and all relationships, is by establishing limits and boundaries that will protect you, allow you to assist loved ones or those in need but which ultimately serve to keep you focused on your purpose. The common theme with *Discernment*, in every situation where it is used, is that it protects, assists, directs and guides appropriately. This is why you shouldn't look at establishing limits and boundaries within family relationships as a negative. Those boundaries are for their benefit just as much as it is for yours, even if they don't realize or understand it. After all, you are the one *Discerning* here so you are the one who fully understands the ramifications of what you are establishing. Remember, the point of *Discerning* is to protect, guide, enlighten and uplift/elevate. You cannot lose sight of these facts. The intent in *Discerning* is never to hurt. Therefore, it's important for you to know that having family as one of your most prized Core Values is not the problem. The problem lies in the failure of you establishing family as a Core Value without establishing boundaries along with it. Having this knowledge now at your disposal, let's understand my definition of family, starting with the family I was born into and how that family dynamic shaped how I navigate through family and other relationships in my life by establishing boundaries from a position of *Discernment*.

MY HUMBLE FAMILY BEGINNINGS

I am number 5 of 8 children born to the same two parents who lived together for a long time but who were never married. In fact, my father was married to another woman when he met my mother. He left his wife for my mother shortly after they met. My parents were both born in the United States as descendants of slaves; they were both Southerners who migrated to the North for better economic opportunities; they sought to escape the overwhelming oppression of the South just as many blacks did in the early 1900s.

My father was born in Ocala, Florida but grew up in Tampa, Florida. He was 1 of 6 children born to a woman who was Indigenous to America and a father who was African-American. My father entered the military at the ripe young age of 17 and retired from the military in his late thirties by the time he met my mother. Upon retirement, my father settled in Long Island, NY and bought a string of stores in a strip mall in Hempstead, NY, one of which was a candy store. He was considered to be a handsome, well established and financially stable man by anyone's standards.

My mom is from Selma, Alabama, the city widely considered to be the birthplace of civil rights in the United States. She is an only child whose mother died essentially in childbirth some 10 days after my mom was delivered by a midwife. My mom's mother hemorrhaged to death due to lack of medical attention after giving birth, a common occurrence that has haunted poor black mothers who had no means of getting to a hospital during the time when my mom was born. Consequently, my mom never knew her mother. She was raised by her grandmother, my great-grandmother, and my great-grandmother's husband, William Johnson.

My mom grew up in a household as the only child. Unfortunately, she was witness to a household virtually oblivious to love, robbed of peace and prone to violence. My mom never heard the words 'I Love You' growing up; and she was the type of child who did as she was told. Understanding her surroundings quite quickly as she got older, my mom focused her sights on getting out of the house one day. And as sure as there are 24 hours in a day, at the age of 18, my mom left Selma on the verge of committing a crime against her grandmother's husband, after he displayed his unequivocal hate for her in a very despicable way. It had everything to do with my mom's desire to complete college. My mom was extremely bright and finished high school early. Upon graduation, she attended the Alabama Lutheran Academy & College. She was studying to become a teacher. The College she attended was several miles away from home, so during the week she would stay at a cousin's house who lived near the College. She would only come home on the weekend to do chores. Whenever she came home, she did her best to stay out of Mr. Johnson's way so he wouldn't beat her like he did her grandmother. My mom was good at listening and speaking only when spoken to. But she and Mr. Johnson never liked each other. One time he had the gall to tell her he wished she was a boy. My mom took most things on the chin but the last straw was when he withheld the final tuition payment she needed in order to complete her last semester of college. This act of hate changed my mom forever and altered her view of the world. Their mutual dislike for one another was out in the open, but there was no way she could act upon it. When it was clear my mom would not be able to finish college, she applied for and obtained a job in New York as a live-in maid. She was happy to pack her bags and leave Alabama for New York with a mere $125.00 she kept in her bra that was given to her by my great-grandmother. My great-grandmother had to slip the money to my mom in secret or her husband would have beaten her. On her way out the door, my great-grandmother told my mom that if it didn't work out in New York, she could always come back home. My mom, however, having this family dynamic at the forefront of her mind, vowed never to return to Alabama and she never did.

My mom landed a job on Long Island as a maid for a Jewish family who lived in Long Beach, New York. These types of jobs were some of the only jobs available for black women in the North at the time. Back in Alabama, my mother's family was cotton farmers and my mom knew she did not want to spend the rest of her life picking cotton from sun up to sun down for only $2.00 per day. She said factories were not hiring at that time and even if they were, her family did not have transportation to get her to and from the factory. So she felt that the best option was to go North.

Housekeeping jobs up North were frequently advertised on the radio in the South and that's how my mom found out about this job. Her new employer paid for the travel expenses, room and board as well as provided her with a salary of $250.00 per week. With this opportunity in front of her, my mom never looked back.

My mom settled into her new life quite nicely. She ended up working for a few families, all of whom were Jewish. She often said that the Jewish families she worked for considered her to be part of the family. She had access to the family car once she learned how to drive. Working for these families was the first exposure my mom had to a family dynamic where she didn't feel unwanted the way my great-grandmother's husband made her feel. She continued working as a maid for about two years until she met my father in 1962. She met my father one day when she went shopping in the nearby Village of Hempstead. On this particular day she went to a beauty salon. Next to the salon was a candy store that my mom walked into to buy a soda. As she walked in the store she was immediately noticed by the owner, my dad. Needless to say, about a year later she gave birth to my oldest brother and my parents' cohabitation culminated in the birth of eight children between 1963 and 1975.

Before my mom knew it, by the age of 35, she found herself saddled with eight kids with a man who was 20 plus years her senior. My mom's dreams of becoming a teacher were nothing more than a distant memory. She was unable to fulfill her career goals and take care of eight children at the same time. This reality caused major problems between my parents that spiraled out of control. If you could conduct a case study on my family you would easily determine that my mom harbored resentment and eventually hatred towards my father that her children paid the price for in the end. My mom unleashed an untamable anger in the form of physical abuse that her children came to expect ritually. While she was careful not to hit us when my father was home, unfortunately, because my father was out of the house most of the time managing businesses, the beatings were quite frequent. Because of this dynamic, my dad was not there to stop my mom from hammering us with the same type of abuse she so desperately sought to escape from during her own sorted childhood. Ironically enough, she came down upon her children because she felt a loss of control over her circumstances. This abuse continued and the resentment and hatred also manifested itself in other ways within our fractured family structure, particularly the relationship between my mom and dad. Eventually, all of her children internalized their relationship in their own way.

While I can recite to you numerous stories of family trials and tribulations that my family endured, what really had a profound impact on all of us growing up was my mom's view of family and how that view was shaped by her upbringing and particularly how she viewed men. Growing up hating her grandmother's husband coupled with a limited ability to love, caused a chain reaction of events that demonstrated how she viewed our family dynamic. This, in turn, influenced how she raised us and how she handled conflict with my dad.

Case in point is one of the worst memories I have of my childhood. When I was approximately 10 or 11 years old, our family was falling apart at the seams. Not only were we evicted from our home and our belongings were literally placed at the curb, we were forced to move into the bottom half of the house right next door on the same street. How embarrassing to have all of your belongings thrown out on the street and then have those same belongings stuffed into half of a house right next door with 11 people living in the house. It became 11 people when my great-grandmother came to live with us after Mr. Johnson died. The house we were evicted from wasn't even big enough for 11 people to live in so now imagine 11 people living in a house half its size??? I just remember all of us sleeping on the floor and on top of one another. We were miserable and it felt like we weren't speaking to one another. My parents definitely didn't speak to one another. Apparently, my father lost all of his businesses and my mom had to go out and get a job. My mom never seemed happy. There was no privacy in the house and my siblings and I were always competing for things and fighting for space. My refuge was getting out of the house and going to school.

So now guess what, just like my mom, when she was my age, I couldn't wait to get out of the house and be on my own. When I got older I would often say 'my siblings were just people I happen to grow up with.' That statement all but tells you how I viewed family. I had no sense of unity, togetherness or a concept of family first. Instead, I adopted the same mindset my mom adopted when she left Alabama. So needless to say, I did not have a moral obligation to 'Family'. Everyone I dealt with, family members and strangers alike, were considered on the same level playing field without any allowances or due consideration given to anyone related to me.

I operated in a rather linear fashion in which I proceeded with extreme caution and made decisions on a case-by-case basis. My character and personality were conducive to this type of reasoning and I functioned this way for years and years until I engaged in needed self-reflection to understand what I was doing and why. And although my family background and how I internalized that background served to protect me tremendously, my concept of family needed to be reset on my terms and not the circumstances I was born into. My logical thinking coupled with the core of who I am was prone to Discern when faced with tough issues. However, I was more inclined to make extreme decisions based upon the traumma I experienced as a child as opposed to making rational judgments rooted in objectivity and facts. So I was Discerning in a hit or miss fashion. This is not good enough for Discernment to thrive and guide. So once I analyzed my actions and beliefs, I began to formulate what I wanted and needed in a family. I also learned the value of family and defined it with purposeful boundaries in order to create the family I desired. I was no longer a stranger to the concept of family; I simply defined it on my terms drawing from my background, experiences, beliefs and goals in the process. Therefore, establishing Family as a Core Value is an avenue for teachable moments in life that help you deal with non-family members and family members alike. That is why the Core Value of Family with boundaries is one of the best core values to uphold as it acts as a breeding ground for Discernment.

But the first thing you need to do is understand your definition and concept of family and know the 'how' and 'why' you developed these views. Let's consider some reflective questions about family.

REFLECTIVE QUESTIONS: HOW DO I VIEW 'FAMILY'

1 - Is Family one of your Core Values? Why or why not?

_____
_____
_____
_____

2 - Describe the Family structure you were born into (e.g., one or two-family household, number of siblings, etc.)

_____
_____
_____
_____

3 - What past experiences shaped your view of Family? Do you recall any traumatic experiences growing up? Explain.

_____
_____
_____
_____

4 - In what ways do you feel you can improve upon your view of Family?

_____
_____

_____

_____

_____

Use these questions to understand what you believe family is and how family has functioned in your life. The next step would be to look at the people you consider to be family and analyze your current relationships with these family members. You will then need to determine how some or all of those relationships may need to change. You cannot be afraid to change, especially when change is necessary for your own personal growth and development.

2 - CORE VALUE - LOVE

Having Love as a Core Value is what I consider to be the greatest of equalizers. I say this because having a view towards Love equips you with the ability to *Discern* with an eye towards kindness, healing and understanding. It also allows you to remove unnecessary bias from your mind. There are so many writings in the world that discuss what Love is and why Love is so important. The Reverand Dr. Martin Luther King, Jr. said it best when he said "I have decided to stick with Love. Hate is too great a burden to bear."

Learning to love is the anecdote to driving out hate, fear, darkness, jealousy and a litany of emotions that take us off the right path. Proceeding from a position of Love no matter what we're dealing with allows us to stay focused on what's important, what really matters. Too often, problems arise because we mistake other emotions for love. We give love sparingly to some and have disdain for others. We walk around constantly looking to benefit ourselves and our loved ones without regard for how we may hurt others in the process. Many of us walk around everyday not knowing how to love because we're operating in survival or 'kill or be killed' mode yet we wonder why we can't seem to elicit the desired responses from people. And finally, many of us find ourselves on the burnt end of an encounter with someone of a different race and that person's race gets blamed for one person's selfish actions. Many of us do not stop to think about how much hate we have in our hearts for strangers because we cannot let go and forgive the actions of a few. It is extremely difficult for love to flow when these are the thoughts that take up residency in your head.

I freely admit that I suffered early on from an inability to display love towards others. If you read between the lines of my family history, you can see how I struggled with understanding what love means. In fact, I struggled with saying the words 'I Love You'. Saying those words actually made me feel uncomfortable. I do not recall hearing those words from my parents when I was a child. It wasn't part of my vocabulary and as I got older, I felt uncomfortable if anyone said those words to me. As I got older, I continued to feel a little uncomfortable hearing those words spoken to me even after I got married and had children. However, I do feel more comfortable saying the words to children than to adults but nonetheless, I still felt a level of internal awkwardness. I am much better now at showing love through my actions than saying the words themselves. But it wasn't until I analyzed why I felt awkward that I began to change my behavior. The goal for me is to lead with love in any situation so that I can see clearly and conduct myself appropriately. This is why I believe love is an equalizer. It keeps you in a space of light and it takes away the cloudiness that you would bring to the table. Love can turn around the most impossible scenarios and turn it into a positive experience and outcome. Leading with Love is a mature disposition that begins with the attaining of wisdom and requires an openness of the heart, your heart. Leading with Love as a Core Value in life stops you from imposing bias upon someone and raises your ability to *Discern* at any time.

REFLECTIVE QUESTIONS: LEADING WITH LOVE

1 - What is your definition of Love?

_____

_____

2 - What does Love mean to you?

3 - Do you express love to all you come in contact with or only to people who you consider to be part of your life?

4 - How do you express love to loved ones? Do you express love to strangers? If so, explain how.

5 - In what ways can you improve upon expressing love to loved ones? To strangers?

_____

_____

_____

_____

_____

3 - CORE VALUE - RESPECT

We discussed the importance of Respect at length in Chapter Two of this Book. What is important to remember about Respect is that it stops you from being on the defensive during your interactions with people, particularly strangers. Treating people, all people, with respect first helps us focus on the purpose of our encounter and not make our encounters a personal test of wits. Also, giving respect to others at the onset of the interaction stops you from thinking solely about yourself and what you need as if you are entitled to something that the person on the receiving end is not entitled to. Respect puts entitlement in its place and makes you keenly aware that the other person or persons you are interacting with matter just as much as you do. Now why wouldn't you want to lead from this disposition? Our interactions would be completely different if that is how we approached people in all situations. We all want respect and, therefore, should give respect to all, not a select few. Giving respect will more than likely result in you receiving respect in return. Even if it doesn't, it will allow you to stay focused on your tasks and not allow anyone else to dictate your actions. If you do not have Respect as one of your Core Values, you should reconsider this decision. Please review the reflective questions on Respect in Chapter Two to see why having Respect as a foundation in your life and during your interactions with people is life-changing.

4 - CORE VALUE - HAPPINESS

If you asked anyone what they want in life, a good portion of people will tell you they want to be happy. But when you follow that answer with the question of 'what would make you happy?' some of those people may not come up with a definitive answer. Why is that? We should all know that happiness is a relative term that means something different to all of us. Happiness at one stage of our lives may change at another stage of our lives. But the reason why happiness is an excellent Core Value to uphold is because it requires you to perform a periodic self-check to determine if you are, in fact, 'Happy'. In other words, you will need to take inventory of your life and what's going on in your life to know if you are happy or not. If something or someone made you happy at some point but is no longer making you happy presently, you need to address it. This type of analysis also forces you to be honest with yourself and, thus, require you to make some changes. Honesty often precipitates change and also helps sharpen your ability to *Discern*. It's that periodic self-evaluation that keeps you on your toes and ensures that you take accountability for your life and your happiness. Most importantly, it stops you from blaming your unhappiness on others because when you self-reflect on the decisions you made, you will *Discern* that you are in charge of your happiness, not anyone else. You will realize that anyone you believe robbed you of happiness didn't and couldn't do it without you giving them the permission or authority to do so. Therefore, without a doubt, Happiness is a critical Core Value for you to have.

REFLECTIVE QUESTIONS: AM I HAPPY?

1 - What does Happiness mean to you?

_____

_____

_____

_____

2 - What makes you Happy in life today?

_____

_____

_____

_____

3 - Are you aware of who or what currently makes you unhappy in life? Please list the people or things that you believe are making you unhappy today?

_____

_____

_____

_____

4 - What is your plan to create Happiness in your life? Does your plan require you to sever ties to certain people or things to achieve the happiness you desire? Do you need to have an honest talk with anyone about your happiness? Explain.

_____

_____

_____

_____

5 - CORE VALUE - SUCCESS

Success is also a relative term that means one thing to one person and something else to another. Success does not necessarily mean being recognized by the masses. Success may mean breaking the cycle of poverty that has plagued a family for generations. It may also mean being a great father to your children when you never had a father figure in your life growing up. Some of us have visions of success early on and take steps to achieve that vision of success. If you haven't done so, now is a great time to start. However, the ones who are able to achieve success do so from a position of being responsible. You become responsible by owning your talents and learning from your mistakes.

Defining your success is yet another reflective exercise that makes you think pointedly. Knowing what you want and what you believe is success helps you stay focused on what you're trying to accomplish in life. Your definition of success may change from time to time and that's ok. It's the act of defining and fine-tuning your definition of success that leads you to knowing what you want out of life. This view of success involves *Discernment* and gets you closer to your true purpose.

As you ponder what success means in your life, *Discernment* will make you aware that looking at someone else's so-called success is not the measure of what your success should be. *Discernment* will stop you from looking at other people for the direct answers to your success. Remember, we find inspiration in others' successes and journeys to success, but we don't use those stories or journeys as the gospel to attaining our own success. This is why any book that gives you a step-by-step guide to achieving success cannot guarantee that you will be successful. That step-by-step guide does not take into account who you are and whether or not your character will fair well with someone else's ladder to success. You may have to change a few steps or even omit a few steps in order for the measure to work for you. The point is that *Discernment* will help you identify the internal steps you will need to take first. We cannot rely solely on external guides that define success on someone else's terms. Success will be individual to you. But first you need to know who you are, what are your strengths and what are your weaknesses. Having success as a Core Value helps you understand yourself in ways you may not have considered before.

REFLECTIVE QUESTION: WHAT IS SUCCESS TO YOU?

1 - What is your definition of success?

_____

_____

_____

_____

2 CRUCIAL CORE VALUES WE SHOULD ALL HAVE

I) Purpose - We all have a purpose for being on this earth, or else we wouldn't be here. The whole point in *Discerning* is so that you can stay on the correct path to finding your purpose in life. *Discernment* eliminates the pitfalls and unnecessary distractions that show up daily to throw you off track. Having purpose as a Core Value should be a non-negotiable Core Value that you need to always keep in mind. Not only will having this Core Value aid you in the *Discernment* Process, but it will also help you see the bigger picture in situations more readily.

Here are some reflective questions for you to think about on the topic of 'Purpose'.

REFLECTIVE QUESTIONS: WHAT IS MY PURPOSE?

1 - Do you believe you found your Purpose in life? Yes/No?

_____

2 - If you believe you found your Purpose, what is it?

_____

3 - If you have not found your Purpose, what do you believe is stopping you from finding your Purpose?

II) Hope - While hope will be discussed more in the Chapter entitled 'Hope and Ultimate *Discernment*', suffice it to say that Hope and *Discernment* go hand in hand. Hope provides the vision of what we want to see happen and what should happen for the sake of humanity. Hope is a foundational Core Value that should be an active partner for each and every Core Value you live by. Hope is generally adapted by visionaries and leaders but is available to all. If you have a lack of hope in any area of your life, you should ask yourself why you feel that way. Here are some reflective questions for you to consider in understanding the Core Value of Hope.

REFLECTIVE QUESTIONS: WHY HAVE HOPE?

1 - What does Hope mean to you?

2 - Have you ever been in a situation where you believe Hope failed you? Explain the situation.

_____

_____

_____

_____

_____

3 - Do you believe Hope is necessary to have in life? Why or why not?

_____

_____

_____

_____

_____

Keep the answers to these questions handy when you review the chapter on Hope and Ultimate *Discernment*.

PRINCIPLES

Standing on Principles as a Foundation for *Discernment*

A principle is defined as: A fundamental truth or proposition that serves as the foundation for a system of belief or behavior or for a chain of reasoning.[1]

Have you ever heard someone say they are doing something based upon principle? If so, that means they are taking a stand based upon something they believe in. They are operating from a position of reasoning. Reasoning is always another great place to start when we seek to *Discern*. Principles serve to give you a basis upon which to make appropriate decisions and choices the same way Core Values do. It is a foundational position with which to start *Discerning*. If you have a set of principles that you use to reason yourself through situations you are faced with, it allows you to follow a logical pattern or course of action to come to a conclusion. If you deviate from the principles you stand on, you will need to clearly analyze why you needed to put aside your principles. Again, the presence of principles triggers an informed/reasoned response instead of an emotional response. You should consider using principles as a way of developing your ability to *Discern*. Doing so makes you more decisive and gives you the confidence you need in knowing your decisions are in alignment with your life goals. Principles can also start out as the guideline to developing your Core Values. Some people use principles and Core Values interchangeably. Nonetheless, both are foundational strategies used to set goals, objectives, find purpose and certainly to help you *Discern* daily.

RULES

<u>Establishing Rules as a Basis for *Discernment*</u>

Rules are either laws, regulations, procedures or a code of conduct that is put in place to guide civil behavior, preserve order and to ensure safety. There are rules you can establish at home; there are rules at work and there are rules/laws enacted throughout society. Where a rule has already been established, the proper way for you to succeed in this situation is to follow the rule. Your assessment need not go any further unless the rule does not accomplish the intended goal or if it creates a hardship of some kind at the point of implementation. However, if the rule was created by another authority and you are either required to follow the rule as a matter of law or if you contractually accepted the rule by using someone's facility, or you're in an employer/employee relationship, then the proper way to confront a problem with the rule is to bring it to the attention of the enacting authority. You making a unilateral decision not to follow a rule that was not implemented by you is not the proper course of action and is certainly not the way you would *Discern*.

The use of oxygen masks on an airplane that we discussed in Chapter Four is the perfect example of why rules should be followed. Using those masks may occur during a life or death situation so it is important to follow the rule so that you will increase your chances of saving your own life and the lives of your loved ones. Rules take the guesswork out of what you should do in certain situations.

Here are some assessment questions you need to consider when establishing your own rules:

1. Do you have a rule in place to follow? If yes, is the rule effective upon implementation? If the rule as implemented is not effective, then there needs to be an immediate evaluation of the effectiveness of the rule? Either the rule should be eliminated or the rule should be changed to make sure it works as intended.
2. If there is no rule in place, establish a clear rule to follow.
3. Stick to the rules at all times.

No matter how you look at it, Core Values, Principles and Rules can and should be used to help you start developing your ability to *Discern*. Start the self-reflection process to determine how you came to believe what you believe. Examine the core values, principles and rules you already adhere to and build from there. You may change certain values and you may have to tweak your self-imposed rules, but having a foundation built on Core Values, Principles and Rules encourages you to begin thinking ethically, logically and objectively so that the process of *Discernment* can begin.

Chapter Six

LIFE LESSONS THAT SHAPE YOUR ABILITY TO DISCERN

Now that you have a functional and practical definition of *Discernment*, and you have examples of how *Discernment* works, you should have a better understanding of what *Discernment* really means. This better understanding, along with your Core Values, Principles, Rules and Boundaries, provide a foundational strategy in which to start *Discerning* regularly. Let us now identify critical areas in your life where you should reflect and improve upon in order to sharpen the lens in which you evaluate the world so that you may learn to start *Discerning* on a daily basis in any given situation or circumstance.

Life Lesson #1
Dispense with the Burden of Selfishness

First and foremost, if you remember nothing else about selfishness, remember this: Selfishness is a burden, not a benefit to oneself. Selfishness is an anomaly of sorts in that you think it does one thing but it actually does another. It's like an anchor that weighs you down causing you to sink. What's interesting about selfishness is that the selfish person believes they are actually getting ahead in life by constantly focusing on themselves, often times at the expense of others. They fail to realize that the more they focus only on themselves and what they want, they are digging a deep hole for themselves that they will not be able to climb out of unless they identify the error of their ways. In the end, selfish people are never satisfied because their self-centered behavior leads to a vicious cycle of focusing on self that goes nowhere. A big part of why selfish people go nowhere is because they will take from others with or without someone's consent. They are what I call 'Takers' because all they do is take from others; they don't give unless they are told or somehow forced to do so. They have not grasped the notion that we were not placed on this earth for ourselves.[1]

Being able to *Discern* starts with the understanding that we were not placed on this earth for ourselves. This is a basic concept that many of us fail to understand. It's not hard to see why this is such a difficult concept for many. After all, as babies we all come into this world operating as if everything is all about us. Babies care not about anything else going on in their parents' lives. That disposition either intensifies or softens depending upon our character and personality traits. It is also further massaged by how we are raised. As we grow older, the extent of our selfishness or selflessness will be discovered outside of our families once we interact with others. For example, whether in daycare or elementary school, a child can and will display a level of selfishness that can be seen and understood by teachers, parents and other children. And then somewhere down the road, we either let go of our selfishness or grip onto it so tightly that it starts the beginning of a stronghold because our wants and desires become the only things we see. That stronghold muffles our ability to *Discern* because we are not thinking of successful, productive and mindful goals; we're only looking for immediate or temporary gratification to please self. Unfortunately, the desire to fulfill immediate self-gratification lends itself to irrational behavior and poor thinking. The decisions made by someone operating on that track may seem like he or she is *Discerning*, but, in fact, because the individual has a narrow focus on what he or she wants in the moment, such an individual will not use all the relevant information at his or her disposal to make decisions that are truly in their best interests. Under those circumstances, the bigger picture is not considered. How this immediate need may affect others is not fully considered, if considered at all, and in the course of wanting something to satisfy self, wants and desires take precedence in the person's life. If you focus solely on wants instead of actual needs, your successes will be short-lived and yet you will continue to wonder why you're unable to reach your ultimate goals or attain lasting success. This is not to say that you cannot choose a want over a need at times in your life, but there are questions you should present to yourself and answer first before you take the step of acting on those desires or wants. A great exercise to incorporate into your life, especially when you have goals you've set out to achieve, is to determine whether something you desire is actually a want or a need. Are there any wants or needs you have that come to mind? Take some time to list your current wants and needs in the chart below:

WANTS	NEEDS

Something is a want if it adds no significant value to your overall goals and objectives in life except that it makes you feel good to have it; it satisfies you emotionally. A need, however, is something that makes sense to obtain because it furthers your goals and objectives and fits into the overall theme of what you set out to accomplish. If you determine that a desire you have is a want, ask yourself the following questions in order to determine how obtaining this want may or may not affect what you set out to accomplish in the short and long term.

QUESTIONS TO CONSIDER WHEN CONFRONTED WITH A DESIRE OR WANT

Pick something from your current list of wants or anything you've had your eye on for awhile that you wanted (it could be anything from $1,000 concert tickets to a brand new car). If you've determined that this is, indeed, a want, ask yourself these questions as part of the analysis to decide whether you can act on this want or not:

1 - What are my short term and/or long term personal goals (e.g., get out of debt, etc.)?

_____
_____
_____
_____

2 - How would obtaining this want at this moment impact such goals? If it doesn't impact your goals, write NONE.

_____
_____
_____
_____

3 - Would obtaining this want affect others, particularly my loved ones, negatively? If so, how?

_____
_____

4 - Can this want be postponed to a later date and time until I've achieved certain milestones or measurable results in attaining my goals?

5 - Will this want add any long term value to my life?

6 - Does obtaining this want have lasting effects that would hinder me in the process of obtaining any of my goals?

. . .

Depending upon your answers to these questions, you may need to forego the want completely, forego the want temporarily or decide to obtain the want immediately without it interfering with your overall goals and objectives. This process is not arduous and will only help keep you grounded as you move forward in developing good habits, achieving goals and identifying when selfishness threatens to derail all the progress you've made.

The purpose of taking the time out to identify wants and needs is to help you become more aware of how you are operating and to make sure selfishness is not the primary reason for the decisions you are making. If it is, a change is in order and that change should lead you into the realm of *Discernment*.

Life Lesson #2
Finding Common Ground in Others

Everyone has their own life story that needs to be told in some way, shape or form for someone else to hear. There is value in everyone telling their story because every life story has meaning and purpose. And within every story, we all experience pain and suffering at one time or another. The act of telling a story can be therapeutic for any person who lived through it because it should serve to free them from the memories of pain and strife the story holds especially when it is untold. When releasing a person's life story into the world, it has the potential to help those who identify with that life story. Inevitably, there is at least one person on the planet who has life experiences similar to yours. So whether it's the storyteller or the receiver of the story, the healing process can take place from both sides once a life story has been told and received. Stories are how we connect with one another. Life stories create connections that defy all physical, racial, social, economic, cultural and any other barriers to basic human understanding so long as we are able to receive it. Often times, stories are the catalyst for attaining human understanding, empathy and commonalities in people who we thought were completely different from us. Finding that common ground through identifying with conflict and pain is a wonderful first step to finding your own way in the world.

For example, you could take a small group of five or six people from different parts of the world, place them in a circle and ask each of them to discuss what they believe are significant struggles they experienced in life. After overcoming any language barriers, I guarantee that all five or six persons can find some common ground in human understanding and relating to one another over pain and struggle. That common ground may come from similar tragedies or adversities they experienced, or it could come from similar family traditions, foods, upbringings, similar dreams and aspirations in life, or other common points of reference that could only be discovered once we converse with one another or through the retelling of our stories. The point is, if we either sat down and had meaningful discussions with people from different backgrounds and cultures, or had the opportunity to read someone's life story and actually listen to and receive it, we'd see that, on several levels, we are a lot more alike than we are different.

The advantage of making this connection is that someone will hear or read another's story and realize that, not only did they experience something similar in life, but that the storyteller may have overcome additional obstacles and was still able to change their situation for the better. Just imagine that someone who suffered a similar struggle such as an abusive parent similar to how you were abused as a child. Now add onto that struggle that they grew up with scarce drinking water and sporadic electricity and inferior education. Yet and still, that person overcame all of these obstacles by forgiving the abusive parent and continued on to finish school, becomes a leader in their chosen industry and established meaningful relationships personally and professionally. Meanwhile, you also grew up with an abusive parent, without the struggle of basic amenities, yet as an adult you are unable to trust anyone due to the parent who abused you. However, after hearing another story of abuse, you now have more information to understand that your situation can be overcome, and it may change your perspective in the process. In other words, that story you connected with can change you and broaden your mind in a way that you did not see or thought was possible before. Perhaps a key piece of the puzzle was your failure to forgive your parent and a failure to release the anger you've been holding onto for so long. This nugget of information can ignite the initial stages of understanding that life is not always what we were fed to believe.

If there is one thing I've learned, it's the fact that there are different ways of seeing and various possibilities that you will not consider if you don't experience a human connection through healing and/or absorbing someone else's story that may have similarities to your story.

Therefore, the goal is to take the positive from your own story and the stories you learn from others and see how they can effectuate positive change in your life. Hopefully, you will search for the commonalities in others first and use those commonalities to begin a process of healing that will open the gate for understanding and thinking on a different level. Once the gate for understanding and learning is ajar, the opportunity for *Discerning* will flow.

Life Lesson # 3
Your Story is Unlike Anyone Else's Story

Now here is the important part in understanding someone else's story: No matter how many commonalities you find in another's life story, ultimately, everyone's story is different. You cannot use someone else's story to completely map out the plan for your life. People fall into the trap of believing that they can use someone else's success story down to every detail and apply it to their lives to make sense of their existence. That is a huge mistake. At some point, our common ground will take a different turn because the more we begin to discuss the specifics of our own situation, the more we will see that each story has a uniqueness all its own. In addition to the uniqueness of each of our stories, each individual themselves will respond to their situation differently according to their gifts, abilities, personalities, character and attitude. So, for example, let's say we meet a person from Timbuktu who endured sexual and physical abuse from their parents the same way we may have. However, the way in which both individuals respond to their abusive backgrounds and how they will use their experiences going forward will be different based upon the unique qualities and characteristics of that person which will determine how that person is able to make sense of their past and how they walk into their future. While one person may use that horrific experience to succeed and overcome, another will allow it to consume them and perhaps hinder certain progress in their life. Again, it is human nature for everyone to interpret situations differently based upon who we are, how we view ourselves and our circumstances in the world. At the end of the day, we either take what has happened to us and allow the situation to dictate our future, or we begin to *Discern* by placing our situations into perspective and move forward by not allowing our situations to impede our ability to move past obstacles so that we may succeed in life. Therefore, understanding our own uniqueness while finding common ground in this world is a balance that we must find and use to our advantage. Appreciating this balance aids in the *Discernment* Process. If you need any evidence of each of our uniqueness, consider the fact that there are billions and billions of people in this world and yet not one of us has the same fingerprint. Every single one of us has a different fingerprint that is not duplicated. If that doesn't convince you that each of us is uniquely designed, I don't know what else will convince you.

Life Lesson #4
Do Not Put Your Emotions in Charge of Your Life!

I've always believed that all emotions serve a purpose. Why else would we have them if they didn't? I believe that the true purpose for emotions is for them to move you in a way that stirs you to look inward, not outward. In other words, emotions are designed for you to hold up a mirror to yourself, first, not to pounce upon someone else. However, that is not what happens most of the time. Either we mistake one emotion for another or we take an emotion to the extreme and now the emotion has lead us into trouble. Think about some of our emotions such as fear and anger. Love is another one. I enjoy discussing 'Love' with my students and during seminars on professional development. I will give my audience a challenge. I say to them 'please explain to me one instance where Love led you astray.' Before they answer I emphatically say to them 'Not one time will that ever happen. And if you think it has led you astray, I guarantee you mistook Love for another emotion. Furthermore, I guarantee that you didn't *Discern* and there was available information telling you that the person didn't love you; this information may even have been staring you in the face.' These statements spark the beginning of spirited discussions that have many rethinking how they viewed past situations and relationships in their life.

The three emotions that many of us tend to confuse, misuse, abuse or find elusive are the following:

1. Love

2. Fear

3. Anger

Let's discuss all three.

Love

We've discussed the importance of Love in Chapter Five and the fact that Love is something we should all be leading with in all of our interactions with people. There is love that you lead with as you interact with people in general and then there's love you give to loved ones or people involved in your personal life. Love is action; it is both a feeling and an action rooted in kindness and confidence in oneself. While it is incumbent upon you to lead with Love, it is also important for you to understand when you do not receive love in return. You must be able to recognize love and know when you must wish others well and love them from afar. But under no circumstances should you respond to a lack of love with hate or anything less than love. Sometimes you just need to withdraw and release. Love is never the enemy.

Fear

Moving on to Fear, there are so many books that discuss fear at length. In particular, I am fond of the book entitled *'The Gift of Fear'* by Gavin De Becker.[2] There are many things I like about this book, starting with the fact that fear is looked upon as a gift. That is awesome and I truly believe that true fear should be looked upon in the positive, not the negative. I will not recite the specifics of the book but it's important for us to look at emotions from a deeper understanding to know that all emotions have a positive aspect to them until we distort them based upon what we want at the moment and based upon our limited understanding of the emotion.

The fact is, we have these emotions as learning tools to help us understand who we are and how we've come to act in the manner that we do. These emotions set the tone for positive change in our lives. Emotions, particularly fear, tell us so much about ourselves. We need to recognize this fact and start a process of understanding why the fear has become a stumbling block instead of a challenge that we take on with our full armor in ready mode. Viewing fear in the positive rather than the negative and using it to address issues inward as opposed to outward is something you should seriously work towards in understanding all the pieces of the puzzle that makes up what is known as 'YOU'.

Anger

Let's talk about Anger. I love anger because I believe anger is the most misplaced and abused emotion we have, even more than Love and Fear. Even though Fear will get us into trouble if it moves us toward acting outward in response to certain situations; it may also paralyze us so we never face fear head on. But anger is probably the emotion that we use most frequently to respond to someone unfavorably. Usually, that response is negative, sometimes even catastrophic, and that's truly unfortunate. What anger should do is propel you to change, probably a 180 degree change that has been brewing inside you for years. Even in situations where it's clear that someone did you wrong without any provocation or malice on your part, what that anger should do is make you sit down to uncover what steps you took to give this person access to you when they didn't deserve it. In other words, even though someone wronged you, the anger is there so that you can work on YOU, not the other person. You should take a step back and figure out where the anger should be placed and devise a plan on how you should handle the matter. But keep in mind that the action plan may require you to leave the other person alone and work solely on you. I know this is difficult to understand but it is essential for peace of mind and upward mobility. You must believe that you are so much better than responding with violence or in a negative light. Use the emotion of Anger in the way it was supposed to be used, to make appropriate changes to self and to stay the course on the way to Purpose.

Life Lesson #5
Learn to Set Boundaries

We discussed boundaries in Chapter Five so let's summarize the top three reasons why you need boundaries in your life:

1. Boundaries force you to take a hard look at all of the relationships you have in your life.
2. Boundaries allow you to stay focused on your destined path instead of running with someone else's agenda.
3. Boundaries help you clearly identify the types of people you allow in your life and which types of people you will need to remove from your life immediately. Boundaries will also help you see these types of people a mile away before they have an opportunity to enter your life.

Life Lesson #6
Let go of *Hubris*, the Ultimate Dreamkiller

Hubris is derived from the Ancient Greek word *Hybris* which means '*Pride*'. I like to use the word 'Hubris' because I believe it conveys the meaning with more intensity than just saying '*Pride*'. Hubris is defined as 'excessive pride or self-confidence; arrogance.'[3] I was introduced to the word Hubris when I began studying the Greek Tragedies and Greek Mythology in college. I always found those stories fascinating. Identifying all the emotions and twists and turns of human interaction along with the presence of spiritual beings was something that has stayed with me all these years.

Of all the elements I've discussed in this book, Hubris or Pride is the sneakiest of them all. Pride is that stubborn mindset that will keep you trapped in a mental prison and will choke the life out of you, figuratively and sometimes literally. Pride will make you believe that you are right and your position should remain, even when you actually see the walls closing in on you. Imagine that picture if you can. Living from a position of Right and Wrong is a sure way to have your life going in circles. That's what pride will do. The Greek Tragedies are lessons to learn from for a reason. With Hubris always being the guiding force in one of the main individual's minds, death was near and certain.

Pride in and of itself isn't a bad thing. We should always take pride in good work that we perform whether it's school work, building something, writing, raising kids, you name it. Pride is a good feeling when you know you are doing good in any area and want to share that good news with yourself and others. There's nothing wrong with patting yourself on the back for a job well done. However, when pride becomes a constant position that is the driving force in life, then the problems begin and they do not seem to stop. *The sneakiness of Pride lies in the warm feeling it gives you; pride whispers to you that you know what's best for you all the time.* What prideful people don't understand is that we don't always know what's best for us especially if we refuse to self-evaluate who we are. Most prideful people refuse to allow any input on how to do something unless it is thrust upon them or it is otherwise a legal requirement that they can't escape. Otherwise, they believe they have the answers to everything. While I hate to say this, extremely prideful people are ignorant, stubborn and illogical. It is painful to watch a prideful person attempt to rationalize their way out of something that makes no sense. Eventually, people leave prideful people alone to their devices until they have to come in contact with them for some reason or another.

I'm not a doctor of any kind but I am convinced that Hubris gains its power over those who somehow had a traumatic experience in life, a traumatic experience that causes something to signal in their brain that they will never allow something to happen to them ever again. Extreme pride takes shape when one is hurting miserably but will not admit it to themselves. At all costs they decide to do things their way even when they know they are wrong. And believe me, there are plenty of times when prideful people know they are wrong but they will stick to their guns anyway. Prideful people often times will not apologize until the dam breaks and the water overpowers the village. If you are prideful and do not get your prideful self under control, you will pay for it in many ways. You will wonder why your dreams cannot come to fruition or can only go but so far. Coming from a prideful disposition means you operate with self-imposed limitations. The mind is only limited to the extent you impose limitations on it and prideful people have the market cornered on mental limitations.

These are just some of the many reasons why you need to take hold of your emotions and not allow them to control your life. Accepting anger as an outward reaction is not going to get you productive results. Allowing fear to consume you and never confronting fear is you being controlled by fear. Saying that you don't know how to love is you robbing yourself of the glorious experience that love offers in all areas of your life. And having pride as your security blanket is really more like you having a snake wrapped around you that is slowing killing you and your dreams. This is not acceptable. You must confront your emotions and take control of them and your life.

Chapter Seven

DISCERNMENT IN ACTION: DISCERNING SAVES LIVES

When I first think about the word *Discernment*, I immediately think about the important role it has played in my life. Without pulling any punches, I will tell you that my ability to *Discern* saved my life more times than I care to remember. And when I say learning how to *Discern* has saved my life, I am speaking in literal terms. I can recall several situations where being able to *Discern* took me out of harm's way. Throughout this book I will continue to share personal stories of *Discernment* that come to mind when discussing salient points on this topic.

Speaking of saving lives, there are a couple of situations that come to mind readily. I remember these situations like they happened yesterday. For example, I remember when I finished all of my collegiate studies and moved back to New York to visit my family and obtain a job. It was the late 90's and racial tensions across the United States were at an all-time high. As a nation, we were still reeling from the 1991 Rodney King incident in Los Angeles where a video captured several police officers, all of whom were Caucasian, beating Rodney King, an African-American male, repeatedly without justification. The matter was investigated and ended with the officers involved being cleared of any wrongdoing; all of the officers were able to keep their jobs. This conclusion fractured the country and left the African-American and certain minority communities feeling more disenfranchised than ever before. And as if this incident wasn't enough, a few years after Rodney King in 1994, the country watched in complete shock as football Hall of Famer O.J. Simpson was chased by the Los Angeles Police Department in a televised real-life drama that damaged racial tensions even further. The chase ensured when OJ evaded police after he was identified as a potential suspect in the horrendous murder of two Caucasians, one of whom was his ex-wife.

O.J. was later tried and acquitted of both murders, an acquittal that set off an even further stifling racial divide and simultaneously set the country back to a climate similar to when the United States Supreme Court handed down the landmark 1954 court decision of <u>Brown v. Board</u>, 347 U.S. 483 (1954). This was the legal decision that ended segregation in schools. Between the riots, rhetoric and injuries that ensured following O.J.'s acquittal, the country was in a state of emergency and needed racial healing. But the failure to charge the Caucasian officers for beating an African-American man, Rodney King, and the acquittal of a African-American man accused of killing two Caucasions, was more like a molotov cocktail of sorts. These two events in U.S. History opened wounds, deepened the racial divide and sparked anger that presented itself on routine encounters between law enforcement and civilians in record numbers. So needless to say, emotions ran high with numerous traffic stops involving minority civilians and Caucasian law enforcement officers.

As a struggling college graduate marred in unspeakable debt, my objective during this restless time in America was appropriately focused on joining the gainfully employed. I had neither a job nor a place to stay at the time, so I kept my priorities on the straight and narrow, as they would say. I was staying with one of my sisters until I was able to afford my own apartment. So one day, after sending out resumes and interviewing with temp agencies, I was making my rounds to see some of my brothers and sisters one uneventful evening. Towards the end of the night I went for a ride with one of my brothers to get something to eat. Here is how our ride began and ended:

Just Cruising on a Typical Uneventful Evening

On this particular night, I was spending some time with one of my brothers. That night, we were driving in his baby blue dodge caravan on the way to get something to eat; the time was around 9:00pm. We were driving through the town we happen to grow up in, a town that twenty years ago was a predominantly Caucasian town. My mom remembers that we were the first African-Americans to move on the block back in the 1970s. Now, fast forward to today in 1998, that same town is now a predominantly African-American town that, over the years, changed for the worse while I was away. Crime went up, schools were not that great and many houses were in bad shape, foreclosed upon or even abandoned. Three of my brothers lived in the next town over so we had to ride through our hometown in order to get to where my other brother lived. We were almost finished passing through our home town, less than a quarter mile before entering the next town when we heard and saw the red and blue sirens in the background. Yes, you guessed it, a cop was pulling us over.

Now before I go any further, let me just say that I have four brothers, all of whom I love, but whom I also like very much. Three of my brothers are older than me. And this particular brother I was riding with is not only the kindest and nicest brother of mine, but he is the nicest man I know. This man would give you the shirt off his back without you having to ask him for it. He has always been well liked by most people so you would be hard-pressed to find someone who didn't like him. If you did find someone who didn't like him, you can bet your bottom dollar that the dislike came from something that had nothing to do with him but more so related to someone's jealousy of him. My brother is a big teddy bear who doesn't like confrontation and always makes people feel comfortable around him. I can count the times on one hand where I saw my brother upset or agitated at someone when we were growing up. And as an adult, as far as I could tell, his disposition had not changed much.

My brother and I were talking about our childhood when the police car came up behind us. My brother was not driving faster than the speed limit so it initially appeared to both of us that the police car came out of nowhere. Once we noticed the police car, and it was crystal clear that he was pulling us over, I looked at my brother and saw the baffled look on his face that quickly turned to frustration and then anger. I admit that I was perplexed as to why we were being pulled over. But at the moment, I was concerned with how my brother, the driver, felt. Then all of a sudden I heard my brother suck his teeth and bang on the steering wheel. Honestly, I could understand his frustration in being pulled over; no one wants that to happen. But as the frustration quickly spiraled into anger, I saw my brother react in a way that I just wasn't used to seeing from him. While trying to find a suitable place in which to pull over, my brother began yelling and getting extremely upset at the fact that we were being pulled over. My brother started saying, "This isn't fair. There is no reason we should be pulled over." He reminded me that he was driving under the speed limit so he couldn't understand what could be the problem here. All in a matter of a few seconds, he started using profanity as his face grew even more angry and he started moving his hands, banging the dashboard and really started to get irate. I actually couldn't believe what I was seeing and hearing. "Who was this man?" was my first thought. Certainly not the brother I knew for 28 years. I know I've been away for awhile, but how could things have changed with him this much? What has the world done to my brother for him to be so upset? I looked at my brother in disbelief. While he was distressed over being pulled over, I, on the other hand, was distressed over his reaction to being pulled over and the police officer hasn't even gotten out of the car yet.

As my brother found a place to pull over, I immediately put my hand on my brother's arm and said, "Listen you have to calm down now. Keep your hands on the steering wheel and don't get upset. Let the officer speak to us and tell us what the problem is." I asked my brother if his license and registration was good and he said "yes." I also asked if he had his insurance card in the car and he again said "yes." So then I said to him, "If everything is legal, then just listen to the officer." I stayed in my seat and my brother calmed down but in one last ditch effort to protest this stop, he said to me, "But I didn't do anything." So I said to him, "Just stay calm and keep your hands on the steering wheel. Let the officer talk first before you say anything." The police car was already stopped behind us now.

It took the officer a few minutes to approach our car. The officer was

Caucasian. I was able to calm my brother down before the officer opened his car door. When the officer finally got out of his car, he began walking over to the van slowly with his large flashlight. I didn't notice it at first but I soon saw that another officer got out of the car and came over to the passenger side of the van where I was sitting; he was also walking slowly with his large flashlight. I stayed still and looked at my brother to make sure he was ok. His face was clearly stressed as the officer walked over to the van but he didn't say a word nor did he move. The officer got to the car, looked in the van and said, "Good evening. Do you know why I stopped you?" My brother, looking straight ahead and not at the officer, calmly but clearly upset said "No, I don't." The officer then said, "Your tail light on the driver's side is out." No sooner than the words came out of the officer's mouth did my brother's face quickly change to a look of surprise; he now looked directly at the officer and said, "Oh, I didn't know the light was out, officer. I just replaced one of the headlights but I didn't know a back light was out." The officer politely said, "Ok. Can I see your license, registration and insurance please." My brother said, "Yes, the insurance card is in the glove compartment." He then reached over me to retrieve the insurance card and then pulled out his license and registration from the wallet he had in his breast pocket. He handed everything over to the officer. The other officer just stood on my side of the van flashing his light in the car but said nothing. After receiving the requested information, both officers walked back to their car and within a few minutes, the one who spoke walked back to the car, gave my brother his documents back and said to him, "I'm going to give you this ticket for the tail light but if you get the light fixed within the next few days, the ticket will be dismissed." In response, my brother, now smiling at the officer, took the ticket and thanked the officer before he went back to his car. The officer said "drive safely", and he went back to his car.

Once the officers got back in their car and pulled off, my brother and I sat in the car, almost as if we were frozen in time. We finally looked at each other for a second or two but didn't say a word. When my brother finally put the car in gear and drove off, we drove in silence. In fact, we didn't get the food we set out to get in the first place. We barely spoke about what happened afterwards. Truth is, we didn't talk for much of the ride after that. It wasn't a long ride since we were near my brother's apartment. There was a lot I wanted to say once the officers left, but I knew this was a situation we needed to let sink in for a few hours or days. And sure enough, it would be a couple of days before my brother and I discussed that night. Thinking about that night, I cannot think of a better situation that shows how I used my individual ability to Discern to guide how my brother handled that traffic stop. I knew for a fact that the stop could have gone a completely different way. It was obvious to me that my brother and I saw the stop from two totally different perspectives and each perspective was going to dictate two remarkably different outcomes. What I do know is that while I was using my ability to Discern, my brother was acting on pure emotion and preconceived notions about why we were being stopped by the police. He did this, despite the fact that we were both raised in a household where we were specifically taught to respect authority. To be more specific, my father was a veteran who had served in the United States Military for approximately 21 years. He was honorably discharged and retired with the rank of Staff Sergeant. My father had passed away on June 18, 1988, 10 years before this traffic stop occurred. I was young when my dad passed, I was 18 years old to be exact. I have very fond memories of my father but a couple of the things that stuck in my mind as I analyzed this traffic stop was the fact that whenever someone came to the house to speak with my father on business, they always saluted him. I also remember that when he died, the military stepped in and took care of everything and was so respectful to me, my siblings and my mom on every level. As a young person at that time, I didn't understand any of what was happening but I know how I was raised and I saw how my father was treated in retirement. Growing up there was no way I would ever think about talking back to an adult or raising my voice in anger or frustration. My mom would have put an end to that real quick. But more importantly, the thought of bucking authority would never enter my mind as an option. This was information I learned at home and I carried it with me throughout every encounter I've had with law enforcement or any authority for that matter. And quite frankly, at the time, I was baffled as to why my brother didn't see the situation the same way as me considering the fact that we were raised in the same household by the same mother and father.

While the concept of Discernment probably did not enter my brother's thought process at that moment in time, for me, the ability to Discern was not a foreign concept or even something that was difficult for me to comprehend. I'm what you would call a thinker. I think, reflect and even dwell on just about everything that happens to me in life, sometimes to a fault. So from that perspective, I have somewhat of an advantage when it comes to Discerning. Although I did not understand that I was Discerning at that moment, when it came time for me to decide what to do when I saw the flashing lights in the background and then witnessing my brother's reaction to the stop, I was Discerning when I advised him what to do as the driver of the vehicle. I gave my brother sound advice by using all the information at my disposal as I Discerned that listening to the officer without first jumping to conclusions was the best decision for everyone involved, not just for me and not just for my brother but for the officers as well. And if the process of Discernment is done properly, you will make a firm decision like that and never look back. You see, my reaction here was based on facts, information and even to a certain extent, the lack of information. There was really only two things on my mind when we were stopped by the police officer:

The police officer is an authority figure, and

I do not know why he stopped us.

These are the facts I know. So with this information in mind, the only logical course of action was for us to allow the officer to speak first before we make any misinformed decisions about why he stopped us. Having in my mind a preconceived notion as to why we were stopped without any other information only serves to complicate the situation. I cannot allow the current climate of racial unrest in the country to dictate my actions. Is the racial unrest something I should be concerned with? Yes, it is something that, as a black woman, I will not erase from my memory nor should I attempt to erase it. However, it cannot dictate my actions. In other words, instances of racial bias and tensions need to be placed into proper perspective. Even though such tensions may be prevalent in our society, particularly when encountering law enforcement, I cannot automatically assume that when I'm stopped by law enforcement that the motive is ill-conceived. If that is how I'm leading, my demeanor will reflect as such and perhaps precipitate a response from the officer that I will then receive as negative. To fill your mind with these thoughts is a recipe for disaster. Do you see the snowball effect that may happen when this mindset is in control? It's like being in a car without brakes; once you put your foot on the gas pedal, you're unable to stop. When you do that in these types of situations, you can't turn back.

> You cannot allow other situations going on in society that you didn't experience first-hand to dictate what happens during your encounters. Remember, the information you received on those occurrences was told to you, you didn't experience it yourself. You must not allow these occurrences to consume your thoughts and thereby dictate how you will respond to situations or circumstances that happen upon you. Look at the contrast between how my brother viewed the traffic stop and how I viewed the traffic stop. My brother discarded facts and proceeded with emotions. Instead of leading with the fact that he did not know why we were stopped, he immediately believed, without any factual basis to support it, that he was stopped unfairly and that he did nothing wrong. So from his perspective, the police officer was already wrong just by stopping us. He didn't even save room for the possibility that he may have done something to warrant the stop. This is a dangerous position to lead from when encountering law enforcement. After the cops pulled off and my brother and I sat in silence, I knew he realized the mistake he made. I, on the other hand, was focused on what would have happened if I weren't in the car with him. But regardless of what could have happened if I weren't there, my brother now had concrete facts to use and negate the preconceived notions he adopted courtesy of the current racial climate in America. You cannot let other people's stories dictate your story. Being fueled by emotions based upon beliefs you acquired from an intangible experience will lead you down the wrong road for sure.

Successful *Discernment* means you make decisions with confidence knowing that you're making a decision that is best for YOU at the time. In addition, if the decision does involve you and others, *Discernment* will help you make the decision that is best for ALL CONCERNED at that moment in time. Another key part of *Discernment* is this: you will feel good about the decision you made because you analyzed it properly.

I don't make it a habit of getting pulled over by the police, but it has definitely happened to me here and there. But whenever it does happen, I am insistent upon keeping my composure during the encounter; this is key. Often times we don't want to admit that the escalation in an encounter with law enforcement is precipitated by our driving status, which some of us are apprehensive about the law enforcement officer discovering. We would like to believe that we can hold everything in and convey what we want to law enforcement but that's not what actually happens. Let's face it, if we get stopped by a police officer and we know we have a suspended license and a myriad of tickets that are outstanding at the time of the stop, we are going to FEEL a certain way. Now, either you are mature enough to face the music and deal with the consequences of your driving status along with the reason why you are currently being stopped OR, the pressure of the baggage you are carrying will somehow manifest itself during your encounter with the officer. More than likely, the latter will occur and the extent of the turnward turn of this encounter will depend on how you handle conflict under these circumstances. However, the mistake we tend to make is to mistakenly believe that we are so smart that the officer cannot see or determine that we are hiding, or trying to hide something. Depending upon how bad your license is, your nervousness, anxiety, anger or whatever emotion is triggered by your driving status, is not being hidden by you, no matter how hard you try. Even if you are good at hiding your emotions, it is the slightest of verbal or non-verbal cues that the officer will pick up on during the encounter. That cue may cause the officer to ask more questions and now you may get frustrated and before you know it, you are angry and now the problem is even bigger than when you were first pulled over. These are factual considerations that may exist before we even get to discuss any inherent bias that may further complicate any traffic stop. No one wants this type of scenario.

Leading with the facts of your situation allows you to put things into perspective without trying to pull the wool over someone's eyes. The truth of the matter is that law enforcement officers are trained in many ways to pick up on potentially dangerous situations. They are by no means perfect people as none of us are, but when you attempt to hide something from them, that tends to create a situation that no one wants. Now please understand that even when you are doing the right thing, there is always a chance that you can be stopped by someone who already has a bias against you. I know all too well how that can happen. However, the best way to minimize being victimized based upon a person's inherent bias is to deal with your imperfect driving status by clearing up your license and any tickets as soon as possible before getting back on the road. By doing this, you alleviate yourself of the added burden of being exposed and possibly jailed, or worse, if you happen to get stopped by the police. Remember, I said minimize, not eliminate being victimized. But again, we must deal with those aspects of a traffic stop over which we have control. That would be our emotions, our actions and our driving status. Another added benefit to clearing your driving record up first is that it will allow you to focus on the actually traffic stop that is before you, not your past and not anything else that is beyond your control. That is how I suggest anyone drive around because the last thing anyone needs is law enforcement judging them on anything more than the current traffic stop that is upon them. And further, I do not need my legal driving status to be an additional stumbling block that may complicate the encounter and give my emotions a reason to rear its ugly head at the most inopportune time.

This all being said, I was recently pulled over by the police in a manner that I felt was not completely kosher. Fast forwarding to a recent traffic stop in 2019 and comparing it to the one where my brother was in the car, I thought sharp and realized that I needed to *Discern* through the encounter cautiously.

Here is what happened:

To Be Right & Dead or Smart & Alive, that is the Question

One day I was coming from a rent-a-car facility on my way to a board meeting. It was the middle of the week and I was planning on going out of town over the weekend. I was a little annoyed because although I reserved a rental a week prior, the facility did not have enough sedans on site the day of my rental and the only type of car available was a minivan. I had no desire to drive a minivan but I was in a hurry and could not wait for the type of car I wanted to become available. So I begrudgingly took the minivan.

My meeting was at 6:00pm so I was driving during rush hour and the roads were packed. I believe I had enough time to get to my meeting on time but I had to switch lanes a couple of times to avoid some traffic on a major highway.

In my quest to switch lanes, I didn't realize at first but I soon found out that an unmarked police car was behind me signaling me to pull over.

So let's make a quick assessment of my disposition before I continue. I'm already upset that I'm in a minivan, I'm trying not to be late for a meeting and now I'm being pulled over by the police. That particular disposition is nothing out of the ordinary and can be anyone's scenario. However, it shouldn't be a disposition that causes you to lose control. My driving status was fine. By that I mean my driver's license is clean and I have no outstanding tickets at the present time. Therefore, there was nothing for me to be worried about besides the current reason why I was just pulled over. The only other piece of information I can think of is that I believe I was not speeding; therefore, I wasn't quite sure what the problem was but, just as I advised my brother years ago to wait until the officer explained why he was pulling us over, I politely pulled over my car to a safe location and waited until the officer approached me with the reason why he pulled me over. At that point I'm not mad; I'm just anxious to get on my way.

When the officer came to my car, he was police and smiled at me. Once again, just like I noticed 21 years ago, another officer walked over to the passenger side of my minivan and looked to see the contents in the van. However, by the time both officers were at the van, I already gained my composure, brushed off the minor distractions of having the minivan and being slightly off course from my board meeting; I focused on the fact that I have no reason to be scared and I should just focus on listening to what the officer has to say. Discernment requires that I do this immediately.

When the officer at my window spoke, he said 'hello' and asked if I knew why I was pulled over. I said "Hello officer. No I don't." He then said, "You switched lanes and did not signal. Is this your vehicle?" I said "No, this is a rental car. I just left the rental office a few blocks down. My vehicle is unavailable." He said "Ok, let me see your license and I'll be right with you." The other officer did not say a word. They both went back to their vehicle and within a few minutes, both emerged from the car in route back to me. When they both got back to my car, the officer who did all the talking said, "Ok, here's your license. Do you mind letting me see what's in that bag you have on the passenger's side." I completely forgot that I even had the bag in the seat. It was my trusty grey book bag I purchased from Barnes & Noble. I carry this bag with me all *the time. The bag contains everything writing related such as books, journals, notes, legal work, my nook, pen and paper.*

So here is where things could have taken a turn for the worse. Need I tell you that as an attorney, I knew that the officer really had no basis for asking or looking into my bag. And if I wanted to, I could have flatly denied this request. But instead of taking that route, I said to the officer, "Sure." I knew the other officer was at the passenger's side so I looked at him first. But the officer at my window said, "No, it's ok, you can just pick up the bag and open it." So that's exactly what I did. I picked up my grey bag, placed it in my lap, opened it and tilted it towards the officer. The officer did a cursory view of the contents and said "Ok, thank you." The officer then said, "Here's your license." And then he said this: "Lisen, we're not just out here trying to give out tickets. We saw you in the minivan with an out of town license plate and you switched lanes without signaling; that's why we pulled you over. We're not trying to single you out. We're sorry. Here's your license and be careful on the road, ok?" I responded "I understand, thank you." I put my bag back on the passenger's seat, put away my license and the officers were gone before I attempted to pull off. But wait a minute, did I just get an apology from the officers who just pulled me over? Why yes I did! But did the officers go beyond what was necessary and proper when they asked to see what's in my bag? Yes, they did. So what's the lesson of what happened here?

I know that how I handled this particular traffic stop at the end would seem controversial to some. I'm quite sure that some people would have been angry and responded differently to the officer once he asked to see the contents of my bag under the circumstances of me failing to signal when changing lanes. The bottom line of what happened is that I used my ability to *Discern* to handle this traffic stop which started out lawful, took a wrong turn but ended in my favor because I used the facts of my driving status, put my emotions in check and kept the end goal in mind to obtain the result I needed in order to stay on the right path. Believe it or not, my goal was not to get out of a ticket; I was thinking well beyond that thought. My intended goal was to continue on my road and not let a distraction along the way become a detour or closed road instead. My vision was securely in tact because I did not let anything or anyone distract me from my focus. Not getting the ticket and also receiving an apology from the officer were added bonuses. You only achieve added bonuses when you *Discern*, keep that in mind.

The wrench in the works was definitely the officer's request to see the contents in the grey bag. But here's a critical fact: <u>my ability to *Discern* dictated that I regard that information as tangential and not information to act upon</u>. I have *Discerned* that my role in this instance is not to be a martyr or make history in this way because I have a different purpose to fulfill. As an African-American, I am well aware of what could possibly happen when I am routinely pulled over for a traffic stop. In fact, look what actually happened here. The officer overstepped his authority; but here's the thing, as an African-American, I do not have the luxury of giving in to my emotions in these types of situations, even when I believe I am right. I do not have that luxury because the end result may prove fatal for me. Now, unless I've determined that my purpose was to die at this moment or go to jail or somehow have this traffic stop take a different turn in order for a lesson to be learned for the greater good, then I would have responded differently. However, I *Discerned* otherwise. Sometimes it's better to be smart and alive than to be right and dead. In this situation, I chose to be smart and alive because I believe God has plans for me beyond this traffic stop.

But you must also understand that someone else in the same situation with the same set of facts as my traffic stop may have *Discerned* through the situation differently because of who they are and what their purpose in life is meant to be. Remember, we are all different people whose purposes in life are all different. This is why when we *Discern*, we are *Discerning* to ensure that we do reach our own purpose in life, whatever that purpose may be. Therefore, because we all have a different purpose in life (and I have no idea what your purpose may be), how each of us *Discerns* in a given situation will dictate a different result or perhaps a similar result in order for us to move closer to fulfilling our own unique purpose.

What I can tell you about this particular traffic stop is that no one should navigate through that same situation and same set of facts by placing their emotions in control of the situation. That I know for sure. Not only will navigating through that situation emotionally ensure a different result, but the result will not be one in alignment with your purpose in life. If you believe nothing else I've said, please believe that.

Essentially, I *Discerned* my way through both traffic stops logically. I navigated myself and my brother successfully through that first traffic stop years ago and I navigated myself through my own traffic stop successfully but differently. However, during both stops, I used *Discernment* to determine how I should respond each time. To do so, I used the *Discernment* Process and it's important that I continue to use the *Discernment* Process as a life tool no matter where I go. You should do the same.

Chapter Eight
THE DISCERNMENT PROCESS

*L*earning how to *Discern* properly means we need to first understand that the act of *Discerning* is a process. The process used in one situation may not be the exact same process used in another situation, but there is always a process. It's also important to understand that, depending upon the situation you are faced with, you may have to *Discern* a situation within minutes or even seconds. It all depends on where you find yourself on the *Discernment Spectrum*. Different situations may require some variation in the analysis used, but when you recognize there is a process, you will know what to look for and you will know where to begin in the *Discernment Process*.

Going back to what I call the Maya Angelou Principle, a breakdown of Maya Angelou's poignant statement also gives us the outline for the *Discernment Process*. Again, here is the statement made by Maya Angelou:

> "When people show you who they are, believe them the first time." - Maya Angelou.

Do you know that this statement has *Discernment* written all over it?

From this statement of *Discernment*, here is what I call the *Discernment Process*:

1. Know who you are; know the person you are speaking with and/or the context of the communication and hear what they are communicating to you.
2. Always listen with an objective ear for the factual information conveyed to you by another.
3. Lead with the facts you have available to you as you digest information received.
4. Accept the factual information received at face value without attempting to alter the information to make it become what you want it to be.
5. Leave your emotions out of the equation when making your initial assessment of what you should do.

I wish I followed this *Process* all my life. But the beauty of the *Process* is that once you know it, you continue to use it going forward and you don't need to look back. This *Process* particularly comes to mind when I think of how I did use the *Process* to stop myself from going down the wrong path. Here is one such example:

The Danger of Being Vulnerable

I remember my circumstances after I completed my law school studies. I had just graduated law school and was flat broke. I barely had enough money to put gas in my old beat up Ford Escort to drive to a friend's house for shelter. My loan money was gone since I had used it all to pay for my food and lodging during the school year as expected. But although my rent was paid up through the end of May when I was set to graduate, I had no more money coming in and I had no job or job prospects. So how was I going to pay my rent for the Summer? My family didn't have any money to give me so there was no one to call for financial assistance. Earlier on in the year, I had decided that I was going to go back to school in the Fall after I graduated law school. I was all set to embark on another degree in the Fall but in the meantime, I needed to figure out how to survive for the Summer. Any scholarships or loan money that I was receiving for the Fall was not at my disposal during the Summer so it was clear that I had a real problem on my hands. I didn't have a place to go until school started in September. So what was I going to do right here, right now?

I loved the apartment I was renting at the time. I stayed there all three years of my law school studies and it served me very well. It was nothing fancy, just a studio apartment in a quiet and beautiful part of town. I was on a full academic scholarship but I still had to take out loans for my room and board. I was diligent with the loan money I received, or as diligent as a twenty something year old could be with thousands of dollars. I believed I did the best I could at the time. So whenever the loan money came in, I paid my rent bill for the entire semester instead of paying it monthly. Growing up we'd been evicted from several homes so I was somewhat scarred and scared of being evicted. Having those memories in the back of my head made me always pay my rent on a yearly basis because I didn't want to worry about where I was living. I used this tactic for all three years of law school and I patted myself on the back for my genius. But now I see there was still a hole in my plan. June came around and I didn't have the rent. In prior years, I was able to obtain Summer loans or I worked during the Summer to keep myself afloat. But now I was graduating and I apparently miscalculated my finances. And despite my excellent payment history with my landlord, like clockwork, the landlord sent out a default notice when I failed to pay June rent by the 10th of the month. Then July came and I received another notice. I started to panic since I still wasn't able to come up with a plan. I didn't want to get put out on the street anymore so I had to think quick.

The default notices came from an attorney's office so I decided that I would call the attorney and get ahead of the situation as much as I could. Maybe I could test out my legal skills and speak to him as an attorney to a future attorney. So early one weekday morning I called the attorney and explained my situation. I focused on the fact that I was never late on my rent in three years of my tenancy and that I needed some time before I could move out. But I reiterated that I was a broke law graduate and I'm actively looking for employment so that I can pay the rent.

To my surprise, the attorney sympathized with me and engaged me on the phone for a few minutes about my studies and my personal life. By the time the call ended, he had invited me down to his office and said he may have a job for me but that he would need to see me face-to-face first before he can decide if I was right for the job. He said he wasn't hiring at his office, but he knew of a hostess position at a restaurant where I could make good money. I never worked as a hostess or worked in a restaurant before, besides my parents' fast-food restaurant when I was young, but I was willing to work there in order to get myself out of debt and keep my apartment until it was time for me to move on. I agreed to meet at the attorney's office the following week during after business hours. It was his idea to meet at 8pm one night. He didn't explain why we had to meet so late and even though I felt it odd meeting someone so late to discuss a job opportunity, I didn't question it at the time. I agreed to meet with him even though something inside me was reluctant to go. Now, before I continue, let me just tell you that if I were using my ability to Discern at the moment, red flags would have been raised about this meeting already. The reluctance I felt was my ability to Discern calling my name; but I digress. The meeting was now set.

The attorney called me a couple of days before the scheduled meeting and let me know that he checked with my landlord about my payment history. He sounded very enthusiastic as he commended me on my payment record and was impressed with my desire to work hard to get ahead. He then confirmed our meeting and while on the phone, he casually asked me to wear something tight-fitting to the meeting; he also asked if I were married or had a boyfriend. I had neither a husband nor a boyfriend and I told him so. Again, red flags should have gone up, but I was way too desperate to see what I was getting myself into at the time. Finally, the day of the meeting came; I was nervous and didn't feel enthusiastic about the meeting, but I scraped up enough gas money to get to the meeting and back home. As requested, I wore something tight-fitting alright. It was a catsuit that clearly showed off all my curves because that's what I was told to do. But I didn't feel right about this. This did not sound like a job opportunity I would ever apply for under normal circumstances, but then again, my current situation was not a normal or ideal circumstance, was it? So, against my better judgment (hint, hint), I pressed on to the meeting. Despite having misgivings all along, I said to myself, "He's an attorney so I have nothing to worry about, right?" As I arrived at the meeting and walked closer to the entrance where the attorney was standing, I noticed he was undressing me from the moment I saw him look at me. He was already in the lobby area waiting for me; he did not bring me into his office. I also noticed that the place was rather dark and there appeared to be no one else in the office but he and I. Once I got close to him, we shook hands as we introduced ourselves and he told me to take off my coat. I complied. Without taking his eyes off me, he told me to spin around and I did. Forget about red flags, sirens and bright lights were blaring and I ignored all of it. At the time, I politely convinced myself that there was nothing wrong with what he asked me to do. Since I wanted a job, I thought perhaps this is how they interviewed for hostess positions, who knows?! He seemed pleased with what he saw and I have no problem telling you that I had a nice figure. I knew I had passed some sort of test because once the twirl exercise was completed, he began to recite the full requirements for the job.

He told me that the job consisted of me being a hostess for a couple of days a week during the day but the real job and money came from being an assistant at night. How interesting?! The assistant job required me to work in the back of the restaurant after hours when the restaurant was closed but there was a social club in the back. He said my job was to cater to the owner of the club as his personal assistant. Serving drinks and appetizers were part of the job, but the main aspect of the job required me to be by the owner's side at the club and to accompany him on any social engagements outside of the club. Then he abruptly stopped talking, looked me straight in the eyes and asked me, "Are you interested?" Without hesitation, I said "yes" and he continued to talk about the position. I allowed fear to answer that question. It was clear that he was telling me something without actually saying what he really wanted to say. That's what Discernment taught me! He kept referring to the position as a 'personal assistant', as if it was the same type of assistant who works in a professional office setting or something. But somehow, I knew my skill of typing 90 words a minute would not be required for this position. That's Discernment at its best.

Then he said something to me that stayed in my head until this very day. He said to me, "This is a great position where you could make a lot of money. The last girl who had this position did okay <u>until she got too attached</u>. She traveled with the boss, received lots of gifts and perks but she got too possessive with him. She didn't understand her place; she started to believe she was the wife and she wasn't. This was a wonderful opportunity for her but in the end, she couldn't handle it. Do you think you can handle it?" At this moment, God knows I should have run out the door and never look back. Hell, eviction is sounding like a great option right about now.

At that moment after he explained everything to me, I knew exactly what he wanted me to be, and I did not want to do it. And honestly, I knew before he made those last statements that he was offering me something I didn't want to do. Who was I kidding? Now, make no mistake about it, I had all the information necessary to Discern what I should have done in this situation. However, I was so scared and in such a vulnerable position that I said to him, "Yes. It sounds great." He quickly followed up with the question: "Are you sure? You need to understand that although you will have the boss's private number, you cannot call him after certain hours and perhaps on certain days. You must stay fit and you may be required to go on trips from time to time. And the money is good." A few more nuggets of information that put the nail in the coffin…even though I no longer needed any further information. But once he spoke about the money, I smiled and confirmed my willingness to go along with the plan. As I smiled, he continued to look me up and down. He said, "Ok, I will let the boss know you're interested and I will arrange a meeting with you and him soon. I want you to think about it real hard and if you are sure this is what you want to do, call me next week; here's my number. I will not schedule a meeting with him until you call me next week. Got it?"

I said "ok" and he gave me a nod of approval. He also said that if I take the position, an important part of the job would be for me to be ready at a moment's notice. I must be available whenever the boss calls. Finally, he said, "Do not discuss this opportunity with anyone." I said "ok," we shook hands and I thanked him. I put on my coat, walked out of the dark office and felt him staring at me until I disappeared out of his sight. My heart was pounding once I got back into my car. I was desperately trying to suppress what just happened even though I knew I couldn't.

After I got back to the apartment, I realized that we never discussed anything about the rent or any time frame for me to pay the rent arrears and move out. I didn't even get a chance to tell him that I had planned to leave town in a month or so, for good. I left his office knowing that what happened wasn't right. Even worse, I knew my response to what was offered to me was not how I would ever respond to something like this. In fact, the real me would never even place herself in a position to hear this proposal. But here's the thing:

being in a state of survival mode allowed my emotions to dictate my responses at the time. After I got home, I thought about what just happened and realized the person who went to that meeting wasn't me at my best. All the warning signs were right in front of my face. Tears came to my eyes and I slumped down on my sofa and drifted into a troubled sleep for the night. And when I woke up the next morning, I gathered my thoughts, started to analyze my current situation and finally let my ability to Discern take over this travesty of events. I was not going to call this attorney back. I needed to devise a plan to get out of my current situation. Why worry, I'm a smart girl.

When it was all said and done, despite my initial lapse in judgment by attending the meeting, I used all the information at my disposal to Discern that this job would not work out in my best interests. And if the process of Discernment is done properly, you will make a firm decision like that and never question your decision. Successful Discernment means you make that decision with confidence knowing that you're making a decision that is best for YOU at that moment in time, but that decision will also have an effect on your future. Another key part of Discernment is this: you will feel good about the decision you made because you analyzed it properly. So how did I Discern myself through this job offer correctly?

First, once I contacted the attorney, I realized that there were two opportunities for me to use Discernment to guide my actions before I actually met with him. The first opportunity arose when I contacted the attorney to try and work out a strategy to amicably end the lease. Just so we're clear, contacting the attorney with the intent to settle the matter was a good move. However, foreseeable problems presented themselves both times I spoke to the attorney before the actual meeting.

The first opportunity for me to Discern that this wasn't something I wanted to get involved with occurred when the attorney wanted to meet with me at 8pm at night. He didn't offer any reason why he needed to meet me so late to discuss a job opportunity and I remember the tone of his voice made me feel uncomfortable. But I decided to ignore these two signs and agreed to meet with him anyway. The second opportunity to Discern presented itself when the attorney called to confirm the nighttime meeting. During the brief call he said two things that should have made me understand clearly that this meeting was a bad idea. When the attorney told me to wear something tight-fitting and *when he asked if I were married or had a boyfriend, I should have known that this was not something I wanted to do.*

Now, I can go into a whole dissertation about why the attorney should not have asked those questions or how sexist those questions were, and on and on. But that's not the reason why I shouldn't have gone to the meeting. The reason why I should have known that this opportunity wasn't for me is because after speaking with the attorney, I knew I did not want whatever job he was offering, end of story. Based upon what he told me in the beginning, twice, in fact, over the phone, before I even met with him, I did not want to proceed with the meeting. In other words, the information I received from him allowed me to Discern that this opportunity was not for me. But instead of relying on what I knew, I proceeded to the meeting anyway. So in that instance, the only thing the meeting did was confirm what I had already Discerned prior. There was no need for me to meet with the attorney because I had all the information at my disposal ahead of time to make the right decision for me. What I did instead was put aside my ability to Discern and allowed my circumstances and emotions to dictate my next steps.

It's mind boggling knowing that I knew I shouldn't have even entertained this idea on any level but I did it anyway. But I am not alone in making this type of mistake. So many of us allow our wants to dictate our actions; many of us allow our circumstances to get us involved in dangerous situations. When we face undesirable circumstances, the feeling of desperation springs forth to speak up for us and we give it full reign over the direction we take. Focusing on the *Discernment Process* will counteract this feeling quickly and successfully.

We must also believe that our current situation is only temporary but the next moves we make can be critical and life-altering. Let your Core Values, Principles and Rules fill your head. You need all of your life tools to stop what could be a tragedy. In my situation, I initially allowed the wrong things to lead me astray, but once I came from the meeting, I knew what I had to do. I could not take this job and I knew it. I just needed to focus on the facts and *Discern, Discern, Discern*. In the end, I came out on top. And in these types of situations, you too can come out on top.

Chapter Nine

DISCERNMENT VS. INTUITION: IS THERE A DIFFERENCE?

Discernment and Intuition are both internal elements that we must tap into as guiding factors in our lives, but the question is: is *Discernment* and Intuition the same thing? The answer is an unequivocal NO! So what's the difference between Intuition and *Discernment*? Here it is:

Intuition

Intuition is based upon a gut-feeling or unexplainable belief or feeling that you should do or not do something. Intuition is not based upon fact or tangible information that you can draw upon in making a decision. On the contrary, Intuition is like a thought that is unexplainably planted in your mind telling you to take a certain course of action without further information. You either act on that feeling or you choose to ignore it.

Discernment

On the other hand, we know that *Discernment* uses facts and information at our disposal which serves to assist us in making rational decisions. *Discernment* is not based upon a gut-feeling or emotion. In fact, feelings and emotions are not part of the equation when one is

Discerning. To be more precise, you are able to *Discern* based upon information that was conveyed to you or experienced by you whether you acknowledge it or not. The information may be direct or it may be indirect (such as body language) but either way, it will lead you to make the correct decision if you utilize the relevant information as part of the decision-making process. When you make decisions using the *Discernment Process*, you will be able to explain why you made a particular judgment and whether each decision is based upon certain information someone said, something you remembered from the past or prior dealings with someone or even non-verbal communication or body language that someone displayed in your presence. The information can also be conveyed as part of an experience you had with someone.

The reason why some people do not *Discern* properly is because they either failed to receive the information that was indeed available or given to them or they chose to ignore the information that was conveyed. Regardless of how the information came to you, *Discernment* takes place in the presence of information. You *Discern* as part of a logical, rational process whereas Intuition requires you to make a decision based upon an internal feeling that steers you in a certain direction.

Intuition does not conflict with *Discernment* because they are two totally different concepts that present themselves at different times in your life depending upon the situation or circumstances you are presented with at the time. They are both important concepts that should be used in life and one does not cancel out the other at any time. These are the primary differences between *Discernment* and Intuition as well as their similarities you must comprehend.

DISCERNMENT	vs.	**INTUITION**
Internal Element		Internal Element
Rooted in Fact/Information		Based upon a feeling
Rational/Logical		Irrational/Unexplainable
Benefits you and others		Benefits you and others

Despite the differences between *Discernment* and Intuition, the similarities between the two cannot be overstated. When you understand what both words mean, you'll know that both *Discernment* and Intuition seek to obtain the same result for you. That is, they both serve to protect and guide you and keep you on the right path. You must start with the knowledge that *Discernment* is a God-Given internal element the same way intuition is a God-Given internal element. Both *Discernment* and Intuition are fruit derived from the Spiritual realm and both are designed to assist you in navigating life so that you may live purposefully and abundantly.

Discernment and Intuition operate similar to the way veins operate in our bodies. For example, within our bodies, we have what is called the 'superior vena cava vein'. This vein carries blood from the head and arms back to the heart. We also have what is called the 'inferior vena cava vein'. This vein carries blood from the abdomen and legs also back to the heart. They are two different types of veins but they serve one distinct purpose: <u>to bring blood from different areas of the body back to the heart</u>. Yes, both of these veins carry blood back to the heart.

Applying the vein analogy to both *Discernment* and Intuition, Intuition operates as a vein that carries unexplainable, irrational and unsubstantiated feelings to your mind and prompts you to act in a certain way. Similarly, *Discernment* operates as a vein that carries factual, rational, substantiated information to your mind also prompting you to act in a certain way. Both are, in a sense, different types of veins that serve one purpose: to carry pertinent information or feelings to your mind so that you will act and make wise decisions that are consistent with the ultimate goal of living out your true purpose in life.

Another point to add when analyzing Intuition and *Discernment* is the fact that both often times specifically remove you out of harm's way or directs you toward an opportunity. When Intuition is the element you are faced with and the goal is to take you out of harm's way, more often than not the danger is imminent. If you ignore the feeling when danger is upon you, the feeling gets stronger. The feeling is like someone tapping you on the shoulder and not only does it not stop but the tap gets harder. When *Discernment* is the element guiding you and the goal is to take you out of harm's way, the information is blaring or screaming at you. The danger here can also be immediate, but often times the danger is somewhere down the road. Since this book details a number of encounters where *Discernment* played an important role in life, let me give you a circumstance where the internal element involved was Intuition and the danger was imminent.

Get Off the Train

The first time I rode a subway was when I lived in London, England at age 22. Once I got the hang of how it worked, I loved riding the Underground and going to different places. It wasn't until several years after living in London that I began living and working in New York City. Of course that led me to ride the New York City subway system. And just like in London, once I got the hang of it, I knew what to do and that was that. But since my family lived on Long Island, on the weekends I would frequently go back to Long Island and stay with my sister and talk about everything and nothing.

Well, one Sunday afternoon as I rode the subway back to my apartment in the City, I was rather tired from staying up all night talking to my sister and I was ready to take a nap. As usual, the subway was crowded but by the time we got closer to my stop in Harlem, the train emptied out. Before I knew it, I was riding the train with heavy eyes trying not to fall asleep. I looked at the electronic subway map which showed that I had about four more stops to go. Excluding myself, there were three people on the subway car, one of whom was a homeless man who appeared to be sleeping on the opposite end of the car as me.

Remember, I am a very observant person in general but I also do not stare. Homeless people are plentiful on the subway so it isn't a shock to see many around New York City and particularly on the subway. And today, this particular homeless man looked as if he was 'out cold'.

When the next stop came, the other two people exited the train leaving only me and the homeless man on the train. Once the two individuals left, I looked over into the next car and noticed a lot of people. Then I looked over at the homeless man and, even though he still appeared to be 'out cold', for some reason I felt uneasy. Oddly enough, even though the subway ride was smooth sailing and the train was not held up by traffic up until this time, all of a sudden, after those two people exited the car and I'm only three stops from getting off, I hear the conductor say the train is being held at the station. He said nothing else.

The train doors were held open and this strange feeling came over me indicating that I should get off this car and go to another car. I tried to brush off the feeling because I was tired and didn't want to move; I told myself that it was only three more stops. However, the feeling did not go away and I felt that if I did not get off, I would be in danger. Now a few minutes passed and I've never known a subway door to stay open this long without further explanation. So I quickly decided to act on the strange feeling and moved to the next car over. No sooner than I got into the next car did the conductor say 'stand clear of the closing doors please.' The doors almost closed on me. It happened just that fast. At first I stood on the train and as I looked at the car I just came from, I noticed that the homeless man I thought to be sound asleep was now sitting up and looked very much awake. I tried not to think much of it. But something also told me to move to another car up, so I did. I settled on a crowded car and felt relieved. This was all a little strange because I rode in subway cars before where it was only me and another individual and I never felt the need to move. I can't say I felt completely safe around a homeless person since I've lived in New York City and seen a few things. However, this homeless man was sleeping, at least I thought so, and I didn't understand why moving was necessary. In any event, now that I moved, the feeling of danger faded and I got off the car at my stop and went about my business.

Later on that day, I was watching the news and learned that the train I was riding, actually not too long after I exited the train, was stopped due to a homeless man who attacked someone on the train. The train was held for an hour or so after the person was able to press the emergency button to call the police, but not before the homeless man struck him in the head with an object. I thought real hard and listened to the timeline before realizing that it sounded like the train I was riding. Then when they showed a picture of the homeless man my heart dropped. It was him!!! I couldn't believe it. I picked up the phone, called my sister and told her what had happened; she couldn't believe it either.

I am convinced that if I did not listen to that inner voice telling me to get off the train immediately it would have been me who was attacked. I couldn't *believe that I considered ignoring that feeling but when the signals became stronger I knew I should move immediately. The subway door must have stayed open at least five or so minutes, and I couldn't get over the fact that as soon as I hopped off and onto the next car, the door closed so quickly. This wasn't the first time I had a feeling coming over me telling me to do something I could not explain, but this particular experience solidified to me why I should never ignore that type of feeling. It was clear to me that my intuition saved me from harm's way. Again, it's a feeling I could not explain with any rational explanation or facts I could rely upon. Instead it was that good ole-fashioned internal element that we all have to steer us in the right direction whenever we need to be protected along the path of life. So you see, feelings are wonderful to have, we just need to use them properly.*

I hope this example and this chapter as a whole helps solidify your comprehension of the differences between *Discernment* and Intuition. Perhaps you can now recall instances in your life where you had unexplainable feelings that prompted you to take a course of action for your benefit. Continue to be in tune with these internal elements so that you can tell the difference between the two and you will be prepared to handle life's challenges and rewards.

Chapter Ten

PERSONAL DISCERNMENT

What we allow to take place in our personal lives stems from several important factors that begin to take shape as soon as we're born. Those initial factors are family structure and environment. As we grow older, these factors are further influenced by our life experiences and the people we are around constantly and how we allow these people to influence our behavior. The people who raise us help shape and mold who we are even though we don't know it. Later on as these factors seep into our thoughts and manifest through our actions, we learn to either hold onto or let go of certain people and behaviors depending upon what's going on in our lives at any given time.

For example, if a crisis arises, we learn to implement temporary changes to fix an immediate problem. However, and more often than not, if there is no urgency or traumatic event that places us on a track to implement change, we learn to accept the familiar and continue our unexamined way of life on autopilot. At the end of the day, most of us only make life-altering changes if we realize that such changes are necessary for our survival or if the change actually asserts itself upon us. In our ideal world, we are mature enough to implement change before a crisis or catalyst forces us to change. But before we start discussing the importance of necessary change in our lives, let us first identify those initial important factors that are responsible for the person we initially become and how it affects our ability to *Discern*.

THE CORE OF WHO YOU ARE

I remember having an intense conversation with a friend and fellow law student over 20 years ago as we discussed things that influenced our lives. At one point in the conversation my friend said to me "The core of who you are will always be there." I am definitely in agreement with this statement. We all have a core or certain characteristics and personality traits that make up a central part of who we are. Even though we may change due to internal and external influences, there are still certain core features that stay with you throughout life. I don't know how many times I've said this but there is no question that the environment we are raised in influences who we are. But we also need to be clear that our core is similar to an imprint or stamp that is unique to each of us.

One of the best things you can do as your ability to *Discern* develops is to be conscious of your core. Being aware of your core means understanding what you like, what you don't like, whether you are an introvert, an extrovert, adventurous, etc. Included in your core is the energy you give off to others. In my case, my energy can be inviting at times and at other times it can signify that I do not want to be bothered.

As long as I can remember I've been aware of my core. I know I'm more of an introvert; I very much like to keep to myself and would prefer to stay at home reading a book rather than going out to drink or party. My husband calls me 'CIA' because I often don't tell him things unless he happens to inquire about a particular topic. One of my sisters would tell me how I always had my nose in a book when we were growing up and guess what? I still always have my nose in a book as often as I can.

A gentleman who was interested in dating me years ago described me as being 'aloof'. That actually sounds about right to me. I dispute none of these characterizations of me because I've performed a great deal of self-reflection to know who I am. I can even remember being in kindergarten and asking my teacher if I could stay inside during recess instead of playing outside with the rest of the class. She usually allowed me to stay inside and I ate an extra snack of Froot Loops or vanilla wafers. She was very nice to me. I would watch her drink tea using hot tap water and it made me want to drink tea. I loved my kindergarten teacher. I was a teacher's pet and one of the students who always cooperated in class. And I would be rewarded for my obedience and I liked that.

But one thing I remember vividly about kindergarten was my grades. When I received my report card, my grades in most categories were mainly 'E' for 'Excellent' except for the category that stated 'socializes well with others'. For that I always received an 'NI' for 'Needs Improvement'. That grade really burnt me up inside. Because I prided myself on getting good grades, I found it hard to believe that I 'needed improvement' in anything. Oh and, yes, my ego was rearing its head at such an early age too. I was convinced this grade had something to do with me wanting to stay inside and not play with the class during recess. I remember thinking to myself, if she didn't want me to stay inside, then why did she allow it? I actually cried over receiving this 'NI' grade for socialization because I felt as if I socialized enough having seven brothers and sisters at home and all. Plus, I got along well with everyone at school so what exactly was the problem? I didn't know at the time but these ways about me were very much apart of my personality and the core of who I am.

Again, while I believe the core of who you are will always be there, as you get older, you should ask yourself if you need to work on improving certain ways about yourself in order to accomplish certain goals. For example, since I knew I wanted to be an attorney, I knew there were minor adjustments I needed to make like feeling comfortable with public speaking. I also knew that becoming a lawyer and teaching required that I be more outgoing and more sociable on some level. Of course I was able to do this, but understand that the core me is still there. Meaning, when I'm not teaching or being an attorney, I revert back to staying at home, keeping to myself, etc. And, again, that's because the core of who I am is more of a reserved, 'speak when I'm spoken to' type of person. But this core has not impeded my ability to succeed in my career or my relationships because I own who I am while still making necessary adjustments when maneuvering in different situations. But in order to do that, you need to have a keen awareness of who you are, what you are trying to accomplish and what is your true purpose in life.

Here are some reflective questions that you can ask yourself about your core and how you handle your core.

REFLECTIVE QUESTIONS: KNOWING YOUR CORE

1 - Do you know the core of who you are? If so, what are the characteristics of your core self?

_____

_____

_____

_____

2 - How has your core impacted your successes or failures in life?

_____

_____

_____

_____

3 - In what ways, if any, have you had to change or somehow alter your core either to fit in somewhere or to pursue either a job, career or opportunity (personal or professional) in life?

_____

The point is, don't be afraid of your core, explore it. Understand it, believe it and don't apologize for who you are. Know yourself so that when you embark on life experiences or deal with people, you will know how to handle these experiences and people. You must know your core.

FAMILY

We've discussed at length in Chapter Five how the family we are born into impacts who we are in many ways. The salient point to remember is that whatever family you are born into, that family structure provides an environment to which you become familiar. This starts from the minute we are born. For example, if you take a child who is born to an abusive mother and by the time the child is two years old, the child has seen and experienced things no child should ever be exposed to in life. For a second let's say the mother has burned and beaten the child regularly and the child is malnourished. Finally, someone calls the authorities on the parent and the appropriate protective agency comes to the home, witnesses the abuses and has a court order to remove the child.

Now here's the part some people will not understand. Even though that child has experienced physical and emotional pain and has not received the proper nutrition while in his mother's care, the child does not know this because this is the only environment the child knows. The child has nothing to compare this environment to, therefore, that child doesn't know the environment he or she is being raised in is actually detrimental to their well being. So at the point the authorities come to take that child from its mother, the child will cry and scream bloody murder because you are taking the child out of the only life the child has ever known. If you don't know something is bad, then it's not bad to you. Ignorance really is bliss until something happens to change your view and you become consciously aware that certain things you've experienced is wrong.

Under these circumstances, you, as an outsider, know that the child is in danger, but from the child's limited perspective, it's simply a way of life. This is why when you get older, you need to analyze your past to understand and digest it and not repeat some of the same mistakes your parents may have made while raising you. Understanding where you come from, what influenced you and then making a conscious effort to view your past is how we learn, gain wisdom and make better outcomes for ourselves. You will also be in a better position to understand that you are not your experiences unless you choose to succumb to them.

YOUR ABILITY TO LOVE

For a number of reasons that can only be explained through self-analysis and reflection, your ability to love also has an effect upon how you interact and relate to people, not just in intimate relationships but with friendships and professional relationships as well. Going back to the core of who we are, some of us are naturally loving and give love to others freely and effortlessly. Others are not so willing to put themselves out there emotionally and are very cautious. Some of us are in between both of these types of people and when they feel the right connections with people, they open up and proceed until someone gives them a reason not to continue. And then you have some people who've been hurt by someone so they convince themselves that love always results in them getting hurt so being alone is the only way to solve this problem. If the person continues on this route, they may one day find themselves alone. If they learn to *Discern*, they will perform critical self-analysis to understand why they feel this way and realize that choosing love is way better than staying on the sidelines of life. Staying on the sidelines of life is a tragic position to resolve oneself to, especially when your feelings about love developed as a child and you failed to reconcile these feelings. Even more tragic, you internalize these feelings to the point of being paralized by them.

I confess that many aspects of my childhood made me afraid to love. By the time I was out of college and came back to visit my family, I flat out told my mom that I would never get married and have children. And everytime my mom visits my house and sees my husband and two kids, she laughs and says 'remember when you said you would never get married and have kids.' My mom always seem to bring this up because I was adamant about never getting married and having kids. I felt this way because I remember being in a house full of kids, never having anything to myself and seeing my parents' relationship turn sour. My parents lived separately by the time I was thirteen and I began living with my father at the age of seventeen. Unfortunately, my father died rather suddenly and that was the last straw for me. In my opinion, my father was the only one who would have helped me through college and in life. In fact, I felt he was the only one who cared about me. The year he died, he died on the day before Father's Day and also eight days before I graduated high school. Having this happen to me set off a chain reaction of events that began with me no longer believing in God and certainly not trusting a human soul.

At the time of my father's death, I wasn't speaking to my mother so I graduated from high school and left for college with some money I had from scholarships I received. I left New York with the clothes on my back. By November of that same year while on Thanksgiving break, I found out that my siblings lost my father's house and everyone was, once again, out on the street. Since everyone living with my father at the time of his death were adults, everyone went their separate ways and began renting rooms. I literally had no home to go to. But since I didn't have any money in which to travel back to New York anyway, I went to South Carolina with my roommate that year.

Since many students didn't have money to go home, I felt relieved that I wasn't the only one; the best part was that I didn't have to explain my sorted past to anyone. The way I conducted myself going forward was to immerse myself in my studies and somehow try to find a better way of life. My concept of family was completely shot. The last thing I was thinking about was being in a relationship or making friends. I was literally trying to survive and simultaneously trying to pretend as if I was ok. But I wasn't ok; I was angry, scared and felt alone. The only thing I knew how to do was get good grades in school and that's exactly what I did. In particular, I loved writing. So everything I felt I wrote down in my writing and poetry classes. That helped me release some of the anger but it was years until I came out of my funk and understood what I was doing to myself. In fact, when I finally felt comfortable enough to explain some of this to a trusted administrator at my college, she took the liberty to explain to me that what happened to me was not my fault. She also explained that it was my responsibility to turn my circumstances around. No one else was responsible for that. I listened and started looking at my life differently. I wasn't a victim, on the contrary, I was a survivor, and it was time for me to get out of survival mode and start living.

What's the importance of all this? You can't go through life believing the whole world is against you and you're fighting all by yourself. You've never win with that mindset. Once I realized this, I put down my guard and stopped withholding love as if it was something I should save for a rainy day. I finally realized that I was capable of love and capable of being loved. We all have this incredible capability and we shouldn't allow anyone or any experience in life to convince us otherwise.

Please refer back to Chapter Five and review the reflective questions on 'Love' and see where you stand with love so you can develop a plan for what you need to do going forward. Choosing not to love will block many things in life; you don't want that to be your script.

TRUST

Keeping in mind what I said about your core self, I certainly was not the most trusting person in the world by no stretch of the imagination. Some people, such as myself, who are naturally loners and who've had certain traumatic experiences early on in life, tend to develop a sense that they cannot trust anyone. I know that's what I did. But again, this concept of being a loner or being an island is not the way to go ultimately. No one's saying that you need to trust everyone who crosses your path. In fact, *Discernment* will stop you from doing that. However, having a mistrust or fear of trusting people in general will manifest itself in various stifling ways in your life. You may lose out on several opportunities and stay stuck in the same rut you've been trying to get out of for years. Ask yourself why you are afraid to trust? This is another area that you must confront in order to make the necessary changes to move forward. Here are some reflective questions about trust that you should think about.

REFLECTIVE QUESTIONS: DO YOU KNOW HOW TO TRUST?

1 - Do you have a hard time trusting people? Why or why not?

_____

_____

_____

_____

_____

2 - Have you ever had anyone betray your trust? If yes, was it someone extremely close to you like family or was it a friend or an acquaintance? Explain what happened?

_____

_____

_____

_____

_____

3 - Do you feel as if you cannot trust anymore because of your prior experiences? If so, why?

_____

_____

_____

_____

Start with these questions to determine the source of your trust issues. The problem with not being able to trust is that you often take these issues out on others who did nothing to hurt you or give you a reason not to trust them. We cannot live in a bubble and not participate in life as a way of stopping us from getting hurt. Being able to trust is an important part of growth. If you have a fear of trusting, you need to deal with it so you can experience more out of life.

FORGIVENESS

Another powerhouse of an issue to deal with is the act of forgiving. One of the saddest commentaries on why we should learn to forgive is the fact that people who don't forgive are more than likely holding something against someone who did something to you and have long since forgotten about the offense. Even better, they may not have even realized they wronged you at all. This person is running around fancy free and you're saddled with the heavy load of holding on to anger, animosity, hurt feelings and emotional pain when it does nothing for you.

If your intent in not forgiving someone is to punish, then I suggest that you rethink this strategy. *Discerners* are not seeking revenge on anyone. As a *Discerner,* you have to make room for the possibility that if you *Discerned* from the onset, the person you have these ill-feelings towards may not have received the opportunity to betray you in the first place. Only you and the other person know the circumstances leading up to you not being able to forgive. Confront and deal with the issue before this becomes a pattern you continue to repeat when dealing with people.

Some people who have problems forgiving often times view forgiveness as a sign of weakness. Coincidentally, these people tend to allow their egos to get in the way of letting go strongholds such as stubbornness, pride and control. Perspective is everything and this view towards forgiveness can wreak havoc on someone's soul. Don't allow this to be your narrative. Here are reflective questions to consider in the area of forgiveness.

REFLECTIVE QUESTIONS: FORGIVENESS

1 - How do you view forgiveness? Do you view it as a positive act or a negative act? Why?

___

2 - Are there currently people in your life who you have not forgiven? If so, why have you not forgiven them?

___

3 - If there are any people in your past or present that you have not forgiven, list all of them.

_____

_____

_____

_____

_____

4 - Can you forgive any of the people included on your list? If your answer is 'no' to any of these people, explain in detail why you feel you cannot forgive them.

_____

_____

_____

_____

_____

5 - If you identified any stumbling blocks to forgiving someone, it's time to understand why? Where do you believe your difficulty with forgiveness stems from? (Take as much time as you need to answer this question).

_____

_____

_____

_____

_____

All in all, you must examine who you are so that you can know why you are who you are and who you want to be. If you are not careful, you can repeat a cycle that continues to run through your family with each generation. You need to learn to ask yourself certain questions without being afraid to find real solutions. You must be willing to dig deeper with the questions because the answers may be rooted in things that happened generations before you were born. Can you believe that?! However, if you don't first look inward to understand your core, how you view family, how you feel about love, whether you have issues of trust and if you are carrying around an unwillingness to forgive, you will not realize how these personal issues affect any relationships you form, how you get along with others, how you are perceived in the world and how that perception affects your life.

TAKE RESPONSIBILITY FOR YOUR ACTIONS

Learning how to take responsibility for your actions keeps you on the road to *Discernment*. When you take responsibility for your actions, you are seeing things more objectively and you are realizing what role you played in where you are in life. So many times I've looked back at certain times in my life when I was stressed out or in a bad situation; I've done this many times to pinpoint how I contributed to my problems. Sometimes it's just one move that can change the outcome for better or for worse. The one move could have occurred when you said 'yes' to someone when you should have said 'no'. Or it could be you deciding to live your life for years without any clear plan of what you are trying to accomplish. It could also be you holding on to your fears and ignoring the opportunities that come your way. Whatever it may be, learning how to take responsibility requires you to look back at things you've done. You shouldn't be afraid to look at the past; you should review your past actions and learn from your mistakes so you don't repeat them. You should also know that until you start taking responsibility for your actions, your thoughts and your words, you will not get to the root of what you need to change, you will stay stagnant, and your ability to *Discern* will be a distant memory.

KNOW YOUR VIEW TOWARDS MEN AND/OR WOMEN

Not too many people will admit or discuss this, but there are a number of people who have negative views towards the opposite sex. These negative views stem from bad experiences we either had as a child or as an adult. For some reason, these views stayed with us and we project them onto others we meet well after the bad experience is physically over. For some of us, that experience could have been ignited by a mother who beat you or a father who sexually abused you. It could be a woman who broke a man's heart after he gave her all he had or it could be a woman who finally divorced a man who cheated on her for years. As a result, that person might believe all men or women can't be trusted and now they will view and treat all members of the opposite sex a certain way that only hinders their ability to sustain relationships.

This scenario may or may not be you, but if you continue to have problems sustaining a relationship, make sure you don't have any underlying bias toward the opposite sex that you have been supressing. If you do, that bias will certainly have an effect on how you deal with the opposite sex personally and professionally. There is so much misunderstanding in the world between men and women that has less to do with the genetic differences between men and women and more to do with our own views that we never admit or confront. Make sure your self-reflection takes this into account so you can purge yourself of this view that, if you allow it, will stop you from achieving happiness in relationships. Ask yourself if you have any negative views towards the opposite sex:

REFLECTIVE QUESTIONS: WHAT IS YOUR VIEW TOWARDS THE OPPOSITE SEX

1 - Did you have any experiences in your past that caused you to develop a negative view towards the opposite sex? Explain in detail the experience(s) that caused your negative views.

_____

_____

2 - What are your views towards the opposite sex today? Explain in detail your current views.

Hopefully you do not have any negative views towards the opposite sex but if you do, self-analysis and reflection will help you make room for different possibilities; it will also help you turn corners to open new chapters that you didn't know were available. You can also create opportunities for yourself because you now hold the keys to the puzzle that make up who you are. You can then move on to productive relationships and begin to think about forging the path you need to walk and not follow a blind path or a path someone else told you to walk. Taking these steps are what sow the seeds of *Discernment* and helps you process information rationally. You will then begin *Discerning* and gain wisdom so that you will make better choices and decisions in life.

THE SIGNIFICANCE OF MR. SPOCK

Finally, to wrap up Personal *Discernment*, I want to give one example of how my core self was in alignment with *Discerning* at an early age. When I look back on certain things I did and certain things I liked to do, I realize that a major part of who I am is a person who typically tries to hold in her emotions. This is how I know my ability to *Discern* was a little more focused than others, even when I did not know anything about *Discernment*. I don't think anything solidifies this point more than my fascination with Mr. Spock.

Star Trek, The Original Series, made its debut in 1966, four years before I was born. I didn't discover *Star Trek* until I was about thirteen or fourteen years old. The first episode I saw focused on some woman stealing Mr. Spock's brain and the crew of the Enterprise spent the entire episode trying to get it back. I don't know if you know anything about *Star Trek*, but Mr. Spock is the half-Human, half-Vulcan first officer who was the captain's right hand. Spock chose the Vulcan way of life over his human side. This meant that he purged all emotions and lived his life logically. I was immediately hooked. I'm not easily starstruck nor do I watch much TV, but this was the one television show I would defy my curfew to watch. It was also the show that got me one of the worst beatings of my life when my mom caught me watching an episode after midnight. I was supposed to be asleep three hours prior but I couldn't help myself. The beating aside, at that young age I had no idea that *Star Trek* was popular nor did I realize it was a phenomenon that continued to grow into a billion dollar industry. All I knew was that I was in awe of Mr. Spock. He was interesting to me because he suppressed emotions and made decisions based upon logic. In other words, he used facts and objectivity to make decisions, not emotions. If he had to guess, he did so using whatever information was available to him. I loved it! I watched intently to follow his logic because my goal was to be more like Spock.

What I didn't know at the time was the fact that the character of Spock and how he conducted himself resonated with millions of people for the same reasons it resonated with me. In fact, I found out that Spock was the most beloved character of *StarTrek*. Why is this significant? I'm glad you asked.

When Leonard Nimoy, the man who played Mr. Spock, died in 2015, the world responded. Even Former President Barack Obama made the statement "I loved Spock." President Obama was not alone. People all over the world showed their love for this particular man and the iconic character he played in many ways. The outpouring of love had to do with the inspiring nature of this character. What people loved about

Spock was his ability to keep his emotions under control and not let them get the best of him. He was the one that the captain would go to for direction and advice because his advice was rooted in logic. To put it frankly, on some level, we'd all love to be more like Spock and respond to situations the way Spock did. I know that's what I wanted to do. And even if we cannot achieve that level of discipline, the fact that Spock's way of living had such an impact on people underscores the level of understanding many of us have when it comes to keeping our emotions in check. We were drawn to this person who has achieved that level of discipline for a reason. He resonated with us because when we think of an ideal better form of ourselves, that better self would include rationalizing our way through the world they way Spock did. There is no question that Spock *Discerned* during every decision he made.

I've had several conversations with individuals on the subject of Spock and the conversations always concluded the same. The importance of Spock is that he reminds us that we need to learn to *Discern* more in all the situations we face in life. We do understand that we cannot purge our emotions completely nor should we try to live life without showing emotions. However, having the knowledge that we need to interpret the world around us more logically will yield us better results in life; we should all continue to move in that direction. Spock is a constant reminder and inspiration for us to think logically and to *Discern* as often as possible. And for that reason, Spock and what he represented, will always be relevant to the topic of *Discernment*.

Chapter Eleven
RELATIONSHIP DISCERNMENT

There's a saying that goes something like *"show me your friends and I'll tell you who you are."* I'm not sure who this statement is attributed to but its meaning is profound. Who we allow the pleasure of our company should be something we think about from time to time so that we can re-evaluate who we have in our lives and why they are there. We don't realize it, but the friends we've had and the individuals we've dated at one time or another were, on some level, a reflection of who we were at that time. Have you ever seen or spoken to someone from your past and after they left you said to yourself: 'How in the world did I ever date this person?' Well, the truth is that you were not so different from that person at the time you were dating. You may have changed since then, but that doesn't negate who you were and what you had in common with this person back then. But if you now look upon that prior relationship in the negative, then the good news is that you are a different person for the better and that's really all that matters now.

There are several reasons why we date who we date or who we allow in our personal space as friends at certain times in our lives. One of the primary reasons has to do with what we believe we need or want at that time. But there are other reasons as well. Often times we allow people around us for a number of unsavory reasons, many of which stem from fear. This fear could be a fear of being alone, fear of making necessary changes or even a fear of the person themselves. But no matter what type of fear we may be operating from, any relationship that is based upon fear, or even a relationship that is unexamined, is detrimental to you.

The truth is, many of the relationships we sustain in our lives are based upon some type of emotional or sentimental attachment and we never really take the time to analyze those emotions to determine whether a relationship is healthy or fatally flawed, that is, until sometimes it's too late. And by too late I mean severe damage has been done to you, the other person and anyone around you who is privy to the relational problems, usually children. Something else to keep in mind is that while you are continuing this detrimental relationship, often times the people around you, insiders and outsiders alike, clearly see what you obviously cannot. It's interesting because the reason why others can see your situation better than you is not because they are smarter than you, but because the lens they are looking through are not clouded by emotions the way your sense of rational judgment seems to be. So you see where I'm going with this, don't you? Clearly your emotions are getting the best of you in several different ways, primarily without you even realizing it.

The outsiders looking into your relationship are actually *Discerning* the destructiveness of your relationship because they have the benefit of interpreting the information that has come to them either from you, the other person involved or through body-language or other information they received, whether they received it intentionally or accidentally. It's a fascinating revelation when we uncover how we all *Discern* at some point in our lives, except perhaps, in the situations where we need to *Discern* the most. For some of us, the problem isn't that we don't *Discern*, it's just that we don't *Discern* when it comes to ourselves.

Unfortunately, when it comes to relationships, emotions are not the only factors involved; relationships are usually not that simplistic. The reasons why we may hold onto certain relationships may be a combination of things, or as I see it, a clash of your emotions with other areas of your life which causes you to shut down and not deal with your destructive relationships head on.

There's no question that navigating relationships can be a daunting task, especially when we fail to recognize when a relationship should end, when another should begin and when to bypass a relationship altogether. This is true whether you are talking about friendships, romantic/intimate relationships, family relationships or professional relationships. There is no doubt that *Discernment* should be used when making decisions in all phases of any relationship but rarely do we *Discern* in these relationships to our benefit. But as we pointed out in the Chapter on Personal *Discernment*, if we fail to deal with examining ourselves and forget to work on the areas where we need to change in order to gain clarity, it will be difficult, if not impossible, to sustain the healthy relationships we so desire in life. So as we discuss relationships, we must keep in mind our attributes, characteristics and early influences in life that help shape who we are and how we interact with others. Once we do this, we can uncover all the elements involved in our relationships and how *Discerning* works or should be at work throughout these relationships in various ways.

FRIENDSHIPS

There is so much to *Discern* when it comes to friendships. Friendships can be one of the most comforting and important relationships in one's life both in times of happiness and in times of grief. I've always believed in the power of friendships, even though I have few true friendships. Just like with other relationships, we look for commonalities when choosing friends. Whether we're in kindergarten and see someone on the playground that we want to befriend or we bond over having the same lunch, it's through friendships that we seek to satisfy our need to connect with one another and share our thoughts, ideas, fears, pain and happiness, among other things. When we're young we have certain needs for friendships and as we get older, those needs change. As people change and experience new and different things, friendships also change. I've had extremely close friends in high school who after graduation, stayed in the same hometown we grew up in and only traveled within a twenty-five mile radius for the next twenty-five years. On the other hand, I left New York at the age of eighteen and traveled the world over the same time period. When my friends and I got together after all those years, it was clear that we had nothing in common any more; things changed since high school. Some of the things they remembered about high school I had long since forgotten but to them the memories were vivid and alive. It soon became apparent that we had little in common since our lives took very different turns. We just weren't the same people and our needs and perspectives changed, some more than others. Sometimes one friend may not want to rekindle a friendship because they may not feel comfortable with what they've done with their life over the last thirty years and may feel even more uncomfortable around you because of what you have accomplished over the past thirty years. This causes the friendship to disconnect quickly. These things happen all the time; times change and some people change with the times. However, the real problematic friendships are the ones in which you feel you're being taken for granted or being taken advantage of constantly.

Friendships can start out in one place and end up on the opposite side of where it started. But truth be told, many of us don't realize that some of the people we may consider to be a 'friend' is actually not a friend at all; when we do figure it out, the betrayal has already occurred and much damage has been done. In those situations, *Discerning* would have alerted you to the reality of the so-called friendship and you would have kept your distance with the person. I love it when a person gets burned by a so-called friend and then resolve that this person was meant to be in their lives for a season. Well, not so fast. What we fail to realize in those types of situations is that *Discerning* would have stopped you from getting burned. Even if the person was someone who was in your friend-circle, it doesn't mean they needed to gain that level of access to your life such that they were able to betray you in the first place. Often times we invite that betrayal because we failed to heed the warning sides because we did not *Discern*.

There were plenty of times where I was in a group of friends and I didn't feel comfortable with one or two individuals. My other friends may not have *Discerned* what I had about the individual so I would politely excuse myself so that I wouldn't put myself in a situation where these people could betray me. Sometimes we need the courage to make the right decision when we have the right information in front of us. We can't just go along with the crowd, allow someone access to our lives, get hurt in the process and then say, well, lesson learned. There are many lessons you will learn in life, that didn't have to be one of them. Remember, *Discernement* doesn't leave you in the lurch. If you *Discerned* that this person was not trustworthy or they just weren't a person you wanted to be associated with, then you could have prevented the betrayal. You must take responsibility for this mishap. The lesson was to get away from the person before they did damage, not for you to allow them to do damage and then you get the message. Once again, this is why we need to *Discern* more so we can identify and avoid these situations.

Friendships are true friendships when the friends mutually benefit from the relationship. You must *Discern* that when a person only calls you when they want something and never call to see how you're doing, they are not a friend. That person is all but saying to you that they are not a friend because the calls only come when they want a need or want fulfilled. I'll never forget my college days, particularly my freshman year when all the freshman settled into the dorms. Some of the students actually had cars in their freshman year. I didn't have a car during my four years in college so I was in awe of anyone who had one. However, I never felt comfortable asking anyone to take me grocery shopping or anywhere because I didn't want anyone to think I was using them. I only rode in someone's car if someone offered me a ride or asked if I needed anything. Otherwise, I was content to do without. I did this because if the shoe was on the other foot, I wouldn't want anyone to only come around me because they wanted the use of my car.

I'll never forget a nice southern girl I met in my freshman year. She had a truck that her parents allowed her to keep at school. She was such a nice girl and I could see some people latching on to her because she was so nice and because she had a car. She was a rather soft spoken girl who attracted one so-called 'friend' in particular who was loud and aggressive; this loud girl followed the nice girl everywhere she went. For the whole freshman year, this poor unsuspecting girl was essentially a chauffeur for the other girl and everyone could see it except her. Some girls even took the bold step of telling her that she was being used but this girl stayed the course and continued to be a friend to this other girl who only called her when she wanted something.

Then one day this aggressive girl got drunk at a dorm party and proceeded to berate the nice girl in front of everyone, including this girl's older brother who was very overprotective of his sister. This girl told her that she was ugly, had no shape, that no guy would be interested in her, and so on. Once her brother heard this, he motioned to his sister to come with him and they left the party. The next day when all the dust settled, the nice girl saw the aggressive girl the next day and walked right past her with a hello and that was it. It was clear that her brother finally got through to her and she realized this aggressive girl was making a fool of her because she was not a friend; she was only using her for the car. And last night the berating was just confirmation of what she really thought about her. The aggressive girl then tried to change her tune and treat the girl differently but it was too late. The cat was out of the bag and the nice girl was not turning back. Luckily the nice girl finally realized that this girl wasn't a friend but look what happened before she figured it out. That's not how it is supposed to work. The nice girl had so many warning signs and opportunities to *Discern* that it's hard to believe she didn't cut the relationship off sooner. It was her niceness that got in the way. It was also too late to implement boundaries so the best solution was to terminate the friendship. But just so we are clear, *Discerning* would have ensured that she avoided the humiliation of having someone say such awful things about her in public. She didn't need to be subjected to that. But because she ignored the information in front of her face, she had to learn the hard way that this girl was never a friend. You should avoid this situation by *Discerning* at the onset. How do you do this? You can start by determining who comes into your life as a friend and who are people masquerading around as friends but who are anything but a friend. In fact, if they are not a friend, just like this aggressive girl was not a friend to the nice girl, here are the three possibilities of who they may be:

1. Haters,
2. Takers, or
3. Pretenders

HATERS

With the help of *Reality TV* and *Social Media*, we should all know what a 'Hater' is by now. A Hater is someone who is not for you; they are against you. Haters proactively try to either steal your light, stop you from getting ahead or otherwise try to stop your progress in life. Haters see the potential in you and they want to take it from you. They would rather see you destroyed and if they can do it, they will. There's nothing subtle about a Hater's contempt for you. They will try to dim your light at every opportunity. Haters are unhappy in life and don't know how to achieve happiness. They are good at identifying other people who are happy and successful and it bothers them. They can even spot people who are on their way to success and they'd rather focus their energy on stopping them from achieving success instead of working on achieving success for themselves. It's actually quite sad because Haters are usually intelligent and they waste their intelligence on being conniving as opposed to putting their intelligence to productive use.

But the secret of a Hater's triumph over you, if you allow it, is the fact that they try to get as close to you as they can in order to cause you harm. This is why you need to *Discern* who are your Haters so that you know who they are but will not allow them into your personal space. Don't just throw around the word 'Hater' as a catchy phrase. Understand what the term actually means, stay away from Haters and learn to surround yourself with people who love and care for you.

TAKERS

This form of enemy does nothing but take from you. While Takers can be anyone, often times they are family members or people you consider to be 'family' and that's how they stay close to you; they only come around or call when they want something. And as we discussed earlier in this book, when it comes to family, some people have a hard time saying 'no' to family, especially if they view family as a top priority. Takers, whoever they may be, will continue to take from you until you have nothing left to take. And if you no longer have anything for them to take, they will drop you as if you never existed ...that is, until they find out that you have acquired more for them to take.

However, if they do not deplete all of your resources, they will continue to use you so long as you allow them. The difference between Haters and Takers is the fact that while Haters want you to lose what you have and do not want you to achieve your goals, Takers have a vested interest in you succeeding because they want what you have. They'd prefer that you continue attaining more because, to them, that means it's more for them to take. This is why Takers will always appear to be happy for you. They may even occasionally bring you something to make you think they care, however, they really don't 'care' for you, they envy you. They soothe their envy by taking from you. You need to stand clear of Takers since they will leave you depleted emotionally and mentally. And if you become down and out, don't count on them to lean on for support. In fact, you will not be able to find them.

PRETENDERS

Of the three types of fake friends, Pretenders are probably the most difficult to ascertain. They are not *initially* trying to destroy you; they are not actively taking from you. However, what they will do is keep tabs on you to monitor your success. They 'pretend' to be friends so that they can stay in the fold. Their hope is that when you make it big, you'll either take them with you or you'll give them some of what you have. They are a hybrid of a 'Taker' and a 'Hater', if you will. They are a little more difficult to spot because they will call to check up on you from time to time without asking for anything. They lull you into a false belief that they care when they only care to the extent that your success will benefit them. They can also see your potential for success, just as the other two types of false friends do as well. They will gather as much information about you to appear interested in you. So long as you maintain contact with them and share what you have with them, they will leave you alone.

However, Pretenders are sneaky because if they continue to check on you periodically and then you achieve success but fail to contact them, they will use the information they acquired from you to then try and destroy you. They'll be the ones who go to the press and you won't suspect it's them because they will continue to stay in contact with you as if nothing is wrong. You can spot a Pretender because if you *Discern* properly and pay close attention, you'll realize that you don't have much in common with them. When they call you to 'check-up' on you, the conversation will be short-lived because you don't have much to talk about. Also, take note of when the 'check-ups' occur. They keep tabs on you to know when good things happen to you. They'll call to make it seem as if they are thinking about you. Well, they are thinking about you alright; they are thinking about the good news they recently found out about you and now they're trying to see how they can benefit from it. Just like 'Haters' and 'Takers', Pretenders can also be anyone such as a co-worker or family, but they are usually someone who you knew early on in life and then you grew apart due to life choices. You must *Discern* that the person you once knew is no longer a friend and, perhaps, never really was.

There are also other categories of people who may try to do you harm such as 'acquaintances'. Acquaintances are generally people who you may have a working relationship with such as at your job, in a social organization or with a community service organization. You should keep a distance from acquaintances anyway so you should be able to pick up on their selfish intentions quicker than the other categories of people we just discussed. It's unfortunate that you must make these determinations about people but the reality is that not everyone is happy about you living a successful life.

So remember to look for the signs of fake friendships and *Discern* when someone is attempting to come into your life for nothing but selfish reasons. You do not need to get into a fight, be humiliated, embarrassed or have a falling out with someone in order to see the light or learn a lesson. *Discerning* is your true blue friend; do not toss *Discernment* aside for anyone. *Discern* in the beginning, not on the back end.

ROMANTIC/INTIMATE RELATIONSHIPS

Most of us remember the first time we fell in love or when we found that 'one true love'. Whether we fall in love in high school, college, on the job, or anywhere in between, intimate relationships are pivotal moments in our lives that can change us forever. When it comes to these types of relationships, it's difficult for me to make the case for us to *Discern* because falling in love is one of those times in our lives when we typically rely on our emotions, especially when we fall in love at a young age. Most young people, specifically kids in middle and high school, are balls of emotion and it's next to impossible for anyone to convince them that a particular person is not the right person for them; it doesn't matter if the warning signs are in bold print. The emotions often run so deep that the ability to reason is nowhere to be found. When this happens, the saving grace will come from the person's upbringing, the core of the person and those unique qualities and characteristics that make up the person.

In my case, my parents didn't say much about dating. In fact, it wasn't allowed when I was in middle school. I dated in high school but, just like most kids, I didn't say anything to my parents. For me, dating was little more than holding hands at school and the occasional going out for a bite to eat. Maybe a Saturday outing took place here and there, but it was during the day and the curfew was strictly enforced. But as I dated, I kept my core, personality and character side by side with my emotions. As I stated before, I just wasn't the type of person to let my emotions take over completely. My personality lent itself well to

Discerning even at a young age and, for the most part, I kept my eyes and ears open to hear exactly what was being said to me in a relationship. This doesn't mean I didn't get hurt, of course I did. No one is immune from anything. The goal is to make better choices in life. In fact, I can recall a particular time when I thought I was in love but *Discerned* that the relationship would not work out for me. I'll never forget what happened back then. Here's the story:

'I Hate My Mother'

I was in high school when I thought I was head over heels in love. I was only sixteen but I felt like I was grown. I was a junior and he was a senior at the time. When we began dating, he treated me the way I thought he should treat me. That is, he always opened the door for me; he always paid for food if we went out to eat, even when I offered to pay; he walked me to class whenever his class schedule permitted; and he took me clothes shopping at times. One time we even went to a jewelry store to look at rings. I thought he was such a gentleman. The ring shopping was a nice touch too. We were too young to be thinking that far into the future, but some thoughts of a future with this man popped into my head at times.

Then one day at school he met me at my last class and asked if I wanted to go to his house after school. I thought to myself 'wow' this is serious. I was nervous because he said he wanted me to meet his parents for the first time. We weren't engaged or anything, but it was still nerve-wracking to meet anyone's parents. I said "yes," of course, and off we went to his house. He must have informed his parents ahead of time that we were coming because when we got there, both of his parents were sitting in the living room waiting for us. I was so nervous I didn't know what to do. As I walked into the room to meet his parents, my nerves got the best of me as I could barely open my mouth to say "hello." His father was smiling at me, but his mother didn't seem too impressed.

Despite the warm welcome from his father and the icy reception from his mother, we exchanged pleasantries and then my boyfriend and I went into the kitchen to eat. If I recall, I believe leftover lasagna was on the menu. After we finished eating, he gave me a tour of his house while his parents were still in the living room pretending to watch tv. The tour went well with my boyfriend saving his room for last. The house was beautiful. He informed me that his room was in the basement; unfortunately, we needed to go past the living room to get there. Leading me by the hand, he politely passed by his parents and took me downstairs to his bedroom. When we entered the room, the first thing I noticed was this huge king-sized bed that seemed to take up most of the room. He told me it was a water bed. Since I never saw a water bed before, I rushed over to see how it felt. And just as we started laughing and rolling on the water bed, there was a hard knock on the door.

We quickly got off the bed and he walked over to the door. As he opened the door, he left to speak with whoever knocked. Within a few minutes, he came back in the room visibly upset and informed me that we needed to go upstairs. Now I was worried that I got him in trouble and his parents wouldn't like me. I got off the bed and proceeded to go upstairs with him. As we opened the door, I saw his mother looking at us with a frown on her face. She look as if we did something wrong. Now I wanted to go home. The last thing I wanted to do was be on his parents' bad side. But we went into the kitchen and started talking about school. After having something to drink and a few giggles, he said he was going to take me home. We went to go say goodbye to his parents and as I turned to leave their presence, his mother said 'I need to talk to you for a minute.' So my boyfriend walked me to his car and went back into the house to speak with his mother. Within a few minutes, he came back to the car and I could tell he was really upset.

We drove in silence for a while but as we got closer to my house, I asked him what was wrong. He parked the car a block or so from my house and we started talking. He began to tell me how he hated his mother and how she treats him like a child. He went on and on about how she interferes with his life and never allows him to do anything. Then he became even more upset as he said, "She lied to my dad and told him that we were fooling around on the bed. I hate her; she's such a bitch." Once he called his mother the B-word I didn't hear anything else after that. I was numb; I wanted to get out of the car. I didn't want him to see my annoyance so I managed to tell him that I had to go home now or I'd get in trouble. He then drove to my house, walked me to the door and we sealed our goodnight with a little kiss. Luckily my mom worked late so there was nothing I needed to explain as I walked into the house.

But after I got settled and began working on my homework, something didn't set right with me about the events of today. More specifically, I was bothered by the conversation I had with my boyfriend about his mother. And the more I started to think about it, the conversation continued to gnaw at me. I knew exactly what was bothering me. It was the fact that he told me two things I wish he never said: 1. He hated his mother, and 2. He called his mother a bitch. I never heard anyone say they hated their mother before and I certainly never heard anyone call their mother any derogatory word, least of all the B-word. Even the way he said it and the look on his face when it was said made me feel uneasy. I was trying to figure out what exactly did his mother say to him that made him this upset. I was lamenting over our conversation for hours until I began crying. I guess this was an appropriate time to show emotion. I was crying because the more I thought about it, the more I realized he and I couldn't be together. The thought that solidified my decision was the stark conclusion that I could not ignore. And that was, **if he could call his mother, the woman who gave birth to him, the B-word, what is he capable of calling me if and when he becomes mad at me?** All it took was this thought for me to know he wasn't the person for me. There was no way I could overlook this information. I made this determination all by myself at the tender age of sixteen. I didn't know it at the time but I was Discerning. Everything about the conclusion I drew had Discernment written all over it.

I was too young to actually articulate or even understand what Discerning was. However, it was clear that I Discerned how this man would probably treat me during our relationship when the going got rough. It's really as simple as that. I also found it quite disturbing that anyone could actually say to someone else how they hated their mother and then call her out of her name. It is possible that plenty of people do this, but the way I was raised, that was a definite 'No No'. Now in the interest of full disclosure, there were a few times during my childhood that I thought to myself, 'I hate my mom.' But you better believe I would never say it out loud, to myself and certainly not to anyone else. In fact, when I did have that thought in my mind, I immediately put it out of my mind for fear that somehow my mother would know what I was thinking and smack me hard. That was the level of fear my mom instilled in me and I was baffled as to why my boyfriend didn't have that same level of fear for his mother. I have seven brothers and sisters and I've never heard any one of them speak that way about our mother either. And although I was convinced

I was in love with this person, I decided in a few hours after he dropped me off that we could no longer be together. We did date a few more months before I ended the relationship because I struggled with the fact that he was always nice to me and how I felt about him. You see how I let my emotions get in the way? But I could not forget how he spoke of his mother. This situation weighed heavy on my heart and in the end, I utilized the information he provided to me to make what I believed to be the best decision for me. I also took note that during the next few months that we dated, he continued to show signs of his feelings towards his mother. Everytime we talked about our parents, I left believing that his father could do no wrong but his mother was the source of all his problems. This consistent disposition being displayed to me was confirmation of what I already knew. And as I recite this story to you, I am confident that I made the correct decision by ending the relationship.

After this experience, which had a profound impact on my development as a young lady, I became even more sensitive to what any man would say or do while we were dating. Essentially, my ability to Discern was sharpened. I used all information that was available to me at a moment's notice. Some of the most important information came from how I saw my father treat my mother; how my brothers treated women, and what men would do and say in my presence. I observed some of the smallest things a man did when I was on a date.

For example, remember in Chapter One I discussed the dangers of making a hasty judgment if a stranger doesn't open a door for you? We discussed the possibility that the stranger may have been having a bad day or perhaps the person just wasn't paying attention as you were coming through the door. Well, when you are dating someone, having your date open the door for you takes on a different meaning because you know the person and you probably expect them to hold the door open for you. So let me tell you about another time when I dated someone and determined that this would not work out for me.

I was out on a date with a man who always opened the door for me. That was important as far as I was concerned because he represented to me that he was a gentleman. And if you believe the man you are involved with should open the door for you as a practice and not simply because the relationship is new, the question you need answered is: <u>whether or not his opening the door for you is part of what he does consistently, or is he doing it to impress you for the</u>

moment? In one instance, I determined that it was being done in the moment when I observed him in action. I noticed that on our first three dates, he opened the door for me. Then one day we were walking into a store and, once again, he opened the door for me. There also happen to be another woman coming up behind us to walk in the same door. However, instead of holding the door open for this woman, I saw him let go of the door and proceed to walk behind me. There was no way he didn't see this woman coming since she was within earshot of walking through the door. I didn't understand why he couldn't hold the door open for her, especially when he specifically represented to me that he is a gentleman. Wow, that really bothered me. And then on another occasion we met at a restaurant because I was coming from a prior engagement. As I walked up to the restaurant door, I saw him waiting for me outside the door. Another woman was in front of me going to the same place. When the woman approached the door, he waited for her to open the door, then he held the door so I could go in. I was in shock! Clearly we have two different beliefs on what a gentleman does. In my opinion, and based upon how I saw my father treat my mom and other women in my family, a gentleman does several things like pull out a chair for women and open doors for women. If a man opens doors for women, he opens doors for all women, not just the ones he date. What was he, a part-time gentleman? Is there such a thing? If I hadn't seen him only open the door twice for me and not for two other women who were right near him, I wouldn't have believed it.

So here's the thing: some women may not have picked up on what he did; others may have picked up on what he did and it may not have bothered them. It may not have bothered them because they may say to themselves, I like the fact that he only opens doors for me. But then you have someone like me who will look at these actions and determine that he is not what he said he is. I say this because if you are truly a gentleman, your gentleman-like qualities apply to all, not some of us. By you being a gentleman only to me, you are telling me that you are only doing this temporarily to impress me, not because you truly believe in holding the door for women as a rule. So in this case, even though he told me one thing, his actions were different from his words. There's a reason why the saying 'actions speak louder than words' rings true. I had to Discern which information was salient, the words or actions. And since I believe actions do actually speak louder than words, I Discerned that he was only trying to impress me in the moment. The bigger picture for me was also the

> question: what else did he say to me that he is that he really is not? You must understand that if someone is untruthful about one thing, they are probably untruthful about other things, too.

I've learned that, whether I'm dealing with friendships or relationships, *Discernment* has never let me down and that's why I'll stick to *Discerning* as often as I can. And by the way, my husband opened doors for me when we dated. During that time, I paid close attention to see if he opened doors for others besides me; he definitely did. And I'm happy to report that we've been married for well over a decade and he still opens doors for me. This is just more proof that *Discernment* is a blessing and you'd better believe it.

Chapter Twelve

DISCERNMENT AND THE NICE-GUY SYNDROME

*I*f there's one thing I've learned in life, it's this: *It's always the thief who locks his door.*

This phrase comes to mind periodically as I *Discern* when dealing with certain people. Unfortunately, there will be people who try to somehow take advantage of you or take something from you that you never offered to them. This phrase also brings to mind the fact that the upstanding and law-abiding individual usually keeps his doors open and gives little, if any, thought to being robbed. Obviously, this is a mistake. And while I am speaking figuratively about leaving the door open, let's be realistic about life; we shouldn't walk around in complete fear that someone is going to steal from us, but we still need to be smart and protect ourselves and our loved ones from predators. There are different types of predators out there but the ones you'll mainly come across are the ones who failed to understand why they were put on this earth so they are content with taking what belongs to you. And if you're a nice guy, they are actively looking for you.

With that being said, let's talk about nice guys. Before we start the conversation, let's be clear about one thing: there is one reason and one reason only why people believe that 'nice guys finish last'. The reason is that some nice guys don't *Discern*. Because the truth is, nice guys who *Discern* do not finish last, they finish strong and they finish in a rather gratifying way. Being nice in of itself is not a problem. Believe me, knowing that you have accomplished your goals through hard, honest work is admirable. And doing so with a cheerful heart is even better. Functioning in the world this way allows you to look back at what you accomplished without the burden of knowing you cheated or injured someone to obtain what you have. But for some of us nice, upstanding individuals, we work hard, not smart. That's another big mistake you shouldn't make. Working smart includes protecting yourself from unnecessary strife and conflict that you invited on yourself. I know that last statement hurt but please do not look at it as blaming the victim for another's bad intentions. Instead, look at it as a call for you to *Discern* more and understand why you are being targeted. More importantly, don't change your positive stance on life; take control over your emotions and actions instead.

It boggles my mind that there are some people who go through life giving out kindness and niceness freely only to get burned constantly. These same people wonder why others continue to step on them to get ahead. Even worse, these nice people continue to give out niceness until one day they essentially give up and determine that the solution to their problem is to stop being nice to people; they change who they are so that people can no longer take advantage of them. Unfortunately, that is not the answer by a long shot.

The quality of being nice is part of that core self we discussed. Being a nice person is not a bad disposition by any means. Nice people brighten up the place all the time. And at no time should a nice person cease from being nice. <u>However, the problem with nice people is the fact that they attract all types of people, I mean everyone: the good, the bad, the ugly and everyone else in between</u>. And unfortunately, the bad and the ugly people see nice people from a mile away and view them as prey. Meanwhile, nice people tend to operate in one gear and don't think to switch gears when they encounter those people who seek to take advantage of their niceness and their kindness. Therein lies the mistake nice people make.

Nice people must learn to *Discern* before they are taken advantage of in any given situation. You cannot operate from a position of one size fits all and expect everyone to respond favorably to you just because you proceed with the best intentions. That would be the result if we lived in a perfect world and we should all know by now that this world is far from perfect. What's interesting is that the people who seek to take advantage of nice people do so rather boldly most times. They size up nice people and are quite brazen with their plot to take from them. To counter this, nice people need to strike a balance between maintaining their good-nature and maneuvering safely through the pitfalls they are subjected to more so than others. In order to accomplish this goal, here are five things nice people should do to stop people from taking advantage of their disposition:

1. Know the person who is approaching you and be conscious of the setting you're in and the context in which you are dealing with people;
2. Listen to the facts presented and *Discern* who is for you and who is against you;
3. Learn to give out information sparingly and only to appropriate people as needed;
4. Implement boundaries; and
5. Learn to just say 'no'.

There's nothing ground-breaking about this list. However, it's a little difficult for nice people to *Discern* because they tend to not have their antennas up. Again, they want to treat everyone with the same level of openness. This is not about respect, because, remember, we should all treat people with respect, right! The issue with nice people is that they give more than is required. And nine times out of ten, they give to people who will continue to take, take, take and take until there is nothing left to take. So when the nice person is depleted, the predator moves on to the next victim and the nice guy is left feeling abused. And if you think long enough about what was done to you, now all the other emotions set in. Now you are going to start evaluating whether you should continue to be nice. But what you're really doing is allowing the taker to control you. In other words, you realize you've been had and now you want to change your good-naturedness. By doing that, you are effectively allowing someone who doesn't care about you, to change who you are. Any changes you need to make in life should be done under your direction. What you should do is pay more attention to what the person said to you. If you focused on what was being said, you would have *Discerned* his/her motives to begin with. Listen, people tell on themselves all the time. You just have to listen to what they are saying. It's really that simple. Remember the Maya Angelou Principle in Chapter Four: "When people show you who they are, believe them the first time." Although everyone needs to practice these five things listed in this chapter as part of *Discerning*, nice people, perhaps, need to work at it a little harder. They need to learn to be more attentive to their surroundings so they can see and understand things for what they really are and not what they wish them to be. Again, they should continue to be nice, but they should be nice with caution/conditions. Here are two examples of situations involving niceness. In one scenario, *Discerning* saved the day; in another scenario, NOT *Discerning* caused the person to get in trouble.

Beat Them at Their Own Game

Earlier in this book, I introduced you to one of my brothers whom I believe is one of the nicest men I've ever known. As I explained before, he would give you the shirt off his back before you even asked him for it. He definitely has an energy about him that is inviting. And the fact that he is easy to talk to makes it all the more reason why people like being around him. But as I also said about nice people, they attract every type of person, good or bad. The ones with bad intentions only care about taking and satisfying their selfish needs. On the other hand, my brother views with people as opportunities to help those in need even though these same people will never reciprocate.

Recently, my brother came into some money and he made the mistake of letting everyone he spoke to know about the money even before he received it. It didn't take long for some people to ask to borrow money. Within a few days, he received numerous requests to borrow money. Once he told me the different amounts, it became clear by the tally that his money was all spent before he ever received it. And here's the kicker, the people asking to 'borrow' the money would never pay him back even though they said they would. They already determined that my brother would never come after them for the money and even if he did, they also knew my brother would never stop speaking to them nor would he actively pursue the money with any level of consistency or enthusiasm. His focus would be more on helping out anyone who needed help.

When my brother told me about all the people who already claimed the money he was to receive, I became angry. What I failed to state earlier is that my brother is physically challenged and he has some health problems that he's dealt with all his life. Therefore, money has always been an issue for him. Over the years, I, along with a few of my other siblings, have helped him out with money. Knowing my brother's situation, I've never, nor will I ever ask my brother to repay any money I've ever given him. And now that he was going to come into some money, I still had no intentions of asking my brother to repay any money that he owed me. Nonetheless, the first thing my brother says to me is "Rhonda, I know I owe you money so I want to give you your money off the top." I told my brother that 1. I haven't kept a tab of how much he owes me and 2. He doesn't need to worry about paying me back. I didn't tell him this but the fact that he has the heart to pay me back is enough for me. You can't get any nicer than that.

I told my brother, instead of focusing on me, let's make sure you are able to receive your money and do with it what you want to do with it. He didn't tell me this but I can tell that he was stressed over loaning money to the people who asked him since they would call him frequently to 'borrow' the money. Hearing the stress in his voice, I gave my brother what I call a 'loving lecture' and reminded him that he has enough to worry about with his health and that he should just focus on getting better. After our talk, my brother had a solution to safe-guard his money. Once he received the money, he wanted me to help him open an account for his money and he would tell anyone who asked him for money that they needed to ask me since I'm the keeper of the account info and I would be the one to obtain the money for them. And with that solution, my brother's problems were solved. This solution is outstanding. Here's why:

While my brother did not tell any of the people who wanted to borrow from him 'no', he simply directed them to come to me for any funds and guess what? No one has asked me for a dime. Do you know why? It's very simple,

I'm nice, but I'm not that nice. I'm very good at saying 'no' when it's necessary. More importantly, the people who wanted to borrow the money knew better than to ask me for my brother's money so they were stopped in their tracks. I haven't gotten one call about borrowing my brother's money, not one.

Now, we can find ways to criticize my brother by saying he should have put his own foot down to just say 'no' to the 'borrowers'; but sometimes it's not that easy for nice people to be that cut and dry. We can't hold someone to another person's standard; what we can do is guide the person to help them make better decisions and that's what my brother was able to do. He did Discern in this situation because he actually utilized number two of the steps nice people must take to protect themselves. My brother knows I am for him, not against him so I would be able to assist him with saying 'no'. It's a step in the right direction and I'll take it. Now he can focus on getting better and not have to worry about dealing with the 'borrowers'. I can deal with them without losing one ounce of sleep at night. This position does not place any additional stress on my plate. If any one of those people did have the audacity to call me asking for my brother's money, I'd politely say no and go about my business. Sometimes you have to beat people at their own game. This is very true when it comes to nice people. If nice people really thought about all the pressure they allow other people to place on them, they'd realize why Discerning will be their saving grace. Think about those five steps I listed and determine how to incorporate them into your decision-making. Here's another story of misplaced niceness.

Being 'Nice' and Fighting for Others

As a parent, learning to Discern with your children is perhaps one of the most difficult tasks that must be done. You must understand each child's personality, core and unique characteristics and navigate them inside and outside the home. You have to know your child's strengths and weaknesses and then figure out how you can protect your child as they grow and interact with society. It starts in the home and continues when the child first goes to school. If you know you have a nice kid, there is no question that you will worry about other kids taking advantage of your child. And when it comes to taking advantage of a child, other children can do it in various ways.

Take my teenaged daughter Nia for example. On one level, this kid's personality is not like mine. She is a social butterfly, she is outspoken and marches to the beat of her own drum. Whereas I was always compliant with all authority figures, Nia ...not so much. With Nia, there was always a story for why she didn't do something a teacher told her to do and it was frustrating for me because the thought of not following a teacher's orders is just not part of my DNA. So this has been something my husband and I struggled with in her upbringing. And since Nia is not of the 'follow the rules' variety, she would often feel picked on by some of her teachers. This made her sometimes feel like the odd girl out. Feeling this way, Nia is the type of girl who would identify and stick up for her friends, especially when she felt they were being picked on. However, she would then assert herself in problems her friends would have and the end result would be that she would get in trouble doing what she believed to be helping out her friends. I cannot tell you how many times Nia would get in trouble for somehow getting involved with a problem that wasn't her problem to get involved with or solve. Whenever I'd explain this to her, her response would be 'but mommy, so-and-so is my friend and this kid was bothering her. I had to stick up for my friend.' The end result would be that she would be the one to get in trouble because she got involved in the situation to the point that she took over the problem and created even more problems. Meanwhile, the friend who was having the problem never seemed to be the one who ended up getting in trouble somehow. How could that be?

What Nia failed to realize is that, although she believed that she was doing good, she was unable to Discern when and if she should intervene in helping another student and to what extent. What got her in trouble was her kindness and willingness to help out those who she believed were unable to defend themselves. But let's just say her method of going about helping others was not compliant with school rules. As her mother, I know the problem is her niceness and her not wanting her friends to feel picked on the way she believes she was picked on. Nia believes she can fight for herself but some of her friends cannot fight for themselves. So guess what? She wanted to do it for them. So now this is where my husband and I have to help her Discern so that as she grows, she will learn not to take on other's problems and get in trouble because of it. And because I know what type of person she is, I can see how later on in life she would be that friend who continues to take on other people's problems and add

> *unnecessary stress to her life. Right now it has caused her to get in trouble at school, but as an adult, the problems may have way bigger consequences.*

As we will discuss in the next chapter on 'Children and *Discernment*', children have a hard time *Discerning* properly. This is why it's important for parents to *Discern* so they can help their children *Discern* correctly. Helping children *Discern* correctly will not happen overnight. You will certainly have to teach them over and over until hopefully they get the message. And hopefully it will not take a catastrophic result before they understand the lesson. And when the child you're dealing with has that nice quality, it may take them even longer to learn the lesson. Therefore, you need to help them through it to ensure that no one robs them of their niceness.

We do not want to look at the quality of being nice as a negative quality that somehow has to be changed. We do, however, should guard that niceness and make sure we give serious thought to being nice with caution.

Chapter Thirteen

CHILDREN AND DISCERNMENT

Are you aware that we start *Discerning* as children? Yes, we actually start *Discerning* and making sense of our existence as our brain develops and our cognitive ability grows stronger. This is why I say, absent any developmental disabilities, we all have the ability to *Discern* and we start doing so early on in life. It wasn't until I had kids and I began telling my mom certain things I experienced with my kids that I realized just how much children *Discern*.

The example that comes to mind is something my daughter did when she was a mere 11-months-old. It happened one day when I took her to daycare. Here is what happened:

When my daughter Nia was born, I was able to take off of work for approximately eight months to care for her. I'm glad I did it. As a mother, I tried to do the best I could during that time to get her on a schedule, nurture her and make sure she had what she needed. Sounds good, right? Well, we all know that raising kids is a challenge. One of the things I struggled with was Nia sleeping through the night just like many moms do. Eventually she got there but it felt like it took a long time before she got it right. Or maybe it took time for me to get it right, I'm not sure. I remember many nights I had to pace back and forth trying to get her to sleep and no matter what I did, it didn't seem to work. I even remember that one time during the day when she was about six-months-old and wouldn't take a nap. Not only that, she cried and cried for what seemed like an eternity to me. I called my mom and she would help me through it; when I got the hang of motherhood, I discovered two things that kept Nia quiet for a good amount of time: 1. Watching Elmo and 2. Having her pacifier.

There's nothing earth-shattering about Elmo and a pacifier keeping a baby quiet. I'm sure many parents have done the same thing. But as far as I was concerned, the pacifier was a lifesaver because it made going anywhere with Nia quite pleasant. I knew that her pediatrician wanted me to curtail the use of the pacifier but as a new mother who needed a break as much as possible, I used that pacifier as if it were a secret weapon. From my perspective, I thought she needed it and couldn't live without it so I let her have it anytime she wanted it. Turns out she wanted it all the time. I told myself that I'd wean her off the pacifier in due time. But as a mom trying to find her way, I found myself going back on my word every time because I was exhausted and it stopped her from crying, end of story.

I began taking Nia to daycare at the eight month mark when I had to go back to work. Every morning she'd come into daycare with her pacifier and I'd leave her in a place where I felt she was being cared for properly. Soon she was 11 months and we were into a routine with the daycare. Nia was walking at nine months so as we walked into daycare by 6:30am, she'd walk directly to the daycare worker who was waiting for her that day.

But on one particular day, I remember we walked in the daycare and Nia's favorite daycare worker was waiting inside to take care of her. This young lady couldn't have been more than 20 years old and I liked her very much. I remember that day; Nia was wearing a white onesie and a cute little jean skirt and white sandals. It was warm out that day and she had her turquoise pacifier in her mouth that, as usual, kept her quiet during the 3.5 mile ride to daycare.

Once we got inside the daycare, a curious thing happened. My little 11-

month old, who couldn't live without her pacifier, I might add, started walking towards the daycare worker quickly. As she walked towards her, she simultaneously took the turquoise pacifier out of her mouth and handed it to the worker. Wait, what???!!!! I'm pretty sure my mouth must have dropped open in disbelief. I absolutely could not believe what I was seeing. So let me get this straight; Nia can actually function without the pacifier? Since when???!!! What kind of hocus pocus magic trick is going on at daycare? I could not believe what I just saw.

My astonishment quickly turned to embarrassment and feelings of failure. I was in my mid-thirties when Nia was born so I was simply beside myself seeing this young girl somehow outsmart me by getting Nia to stop using the pacifier without her throwing some sort of tantrum. Meanwhile, the young lady smiled and said a big 'Thank You Nia!' and Nia walked right on into the playroom ready for the activities of the day. She didn't even look back at me; she was gone.

What I just witnessed with my own eyes really bothered me because I didn't understand at the time that my 11-month-old baby *Discerned* that with me she could get away with having that pacifier as long as she wanted but at daycare they were having none of it. Nia knew that they were going to take the pacifier out of her mouth and no amount of crying was going to change that reality. Knowing this, she was proactive and removed that pacifier from her mouth as soon as she walked in the door and I didn't see a tear in sight. Honestly, I felt like a fool. This was a sobering moment for me as a mother. But this made me realize that even as early as 11-months-old, and perhaps even before then, children are learning and *Discerning*. This particular situation bothered me so much that I actually went to the manager and asked how she was able to accomplish this task that seemed so unattainable to me.

She explained that the daycare has a strict routine and policy which includes a no pacifier rule. Sanitary reasons was the first consideration. But also, their goal was to engage the children's senses and focus on developing their motor and neurological skills. Pacifiers did not fit into the plan so if a child comes to the center with one, they take it away and put it in the child's diaper bag for the parents. They do not make any exceptions with respect to the use of pacifiers. This was mind-blowing to me but it bothered me that I felt I couldn't do this at home. Overall, there was a lesson to be learned and it has to do with how children learn to adapt to their environment. Often times they get what they want but it doesn't have to be that way all the time. The level of discipline we apply as parents has an effect on them. Many times our lives are cluttered with so many things that we do not have time to enforce rules and foster disciple in ways that we should. What a valuable lesson I learned that day.

My mom would always say to me 'kids are smarter than we give them credit for.' Boy was she right. I accept this statement as true and I understand what my mom meant by this statement. She was telling me that children learn to *Discern* and maneuver in different ways to get what they want. We would never consider what children do to get what they want as *Discernment* because they are proceeding from a natural position of selfishness. But as children, that's how they will function until they grow and, hopefully, learn the concept of doing for others, sharing and other aspects of life that will help shape the type of person they will grow into as adults.

The primary way children *Discern* at a very young age is when they are with their parents. Children *Discern* as they determine which parent will give them what they want and which parent will not. Children also know which parent they can push to their limits and which parent has them on a shorter leash. Understanding how children perceive their parents' roles becomes evident by the way children interact with their mothers and fathers. Children tend to act one way around their father and another way around their mother. There is research in this area that addresses the way children respond to females and how they respond to males. These responses have to do with the distinct differences between men and women and how easily children comprehend and adapt to those differences. For example, children learn that one parent may allow candy before dinner and another parent may not. So guess which parent they will go to for candy? Also, generally speaking, women tend to have more patience with children and may tolerate a child's bad behavior more so than men. There are numerous factors involved when analyzing how men and women deal with children besides the inherent differences between men and women. There are also the unique personal qualities each of us bring to the table. And you need to know that children soak up all of these differences and will exploit them to their advantage as early and as often as they can.

Children are constantly assessing their parents to know which parent needs a backstory or condition fulfilled before they can receive something they want. And they do this based upon what they've learned through interacting with their parents and, more importantly, what we show them. Children *Discern* within their limited environment for the purposes of getting what they want. In order to do this, they figure out who to divulge unpleasant information to first without getting into trouble and they learn how to position a situation to a parent when they want something. In other words, they can be strategic when they want to achieve a desired result from their parents. For example, my teenager has chores that she has to perform daily such as cleaning her room, making her bed every morning before leaving the house and also completing her homework first before participating in any social engagements with friends.

Although she knows these things must be done, just about every night I have to check and specifically ask her if these chores are actually completed. However, if on a particular day there is a birthday party or a friend get-together happening, out of nowhere you will hear the vacuum blaring in my house, dishes being washed, clothes being washed and at some point my daughter will tell me that her homework is already done. She will do this all on her own initiative because something is at stake. Then all of a sudden she'll come back into my room to say 'Hi mommy. How was your day? I cleaned up my room, swept the floor, vacuumed, laid out my clothes for tomorrow, washed the dishes and you already know I did my homework.' She makes sure I'm aware that some of the things she completed were extra things she did on top of her required chores. Now of course I already *Discerned* that she wanted something as soon as I heard the vacuum going, but more importantly, she *Discerned* that before she can even ask me about doing something, the chores must be done; she also let it be known that she went the extra mile as well. In other words, she figured me out and she believes what she knows about me. Once again, the Maya Angelou Principle applies here. Nia knows that I will not even entertain her doing anything until those chores are done. She also knows that if she even asks to do something before she completes the chores, I would flat out say 'no!' Therefore, because of what she *Discerned* about me and because she wants something from me, she will complete the chores without me asking and will complete additional tasks as added insurance so that I know she went above and beyond what was expected of her. You gotta love it. How could you not?!

My daughter isn't the only child who does this. In fact, many children do this; some may be better at it than others, but many children try their hand at it. Of course when my daughter does it I still take the liberty to opine on the fact that she does this only when she wants something and that she should do this everyday. But in the end, after her performance, I will probably let her go with her friends and she knows this. Now if I wasn't home that day and my husband was the one at home, her approach would have been totally different because she also *Discerned* how he would respond to her request. First, she wouldn't have even completed her regular chores because she knows my husband would not have asked about them. In fact, my daughter would have just asked my husband if she could go out with her friends. She probably would have offered the information about her homework being done and that would have been all she offered. And then she would have been able to go out with her friends to socialize, something my daughter loves to do.

Any of her strategic efforts would have been accomplished through *Discernment*. She used the information she knows of me to position herself to obtain a particular result. This is a classic way of how children *Discern*. However, the caveat when children *Discern* is that, although their *Discernment* is based upon information they gain through their environment, their end goal is almost always to satisfy self. Therefore, because they *Discern* for selfish reasons, their use of the information at their disposal may not always get them what they want.

What do I mean by that? Remember, since we already know that when adults operate from a selfish disposition, it ultimately backfires on them because, in the long run, selfishness doesn't get us where we want to be in life. Well, the same is true when children act in selfish ways. However, the difference is that as adults, to a certain extent, we expect children to behave selfishly because they are children and that's what children do. So we know they are going to use information selfishly. But as adults, we should know better than to live and act selfishly as a way of life. As adults, we should know that being selfish will lead nowhere whereas when it comes to our children, we can use their selfish ways as teachable moments to help them process information better so they can eventually do better. Therefore, we cannot fully expect children to utilize the information they receive as maturely as we do until we teach them accordingly.

So while we understand that a child's ability to *Discern* is usually done so selfishly, we must also understand that if they get older and continue to process information for selfish gain, they will not be able to achieve the results they are looking for and they will certainly not be fulfilled in life. This is true because we now know that *Discernment* is an ability used purposefully and maturely and not for ill-gain. Therefore, allowing selfishness to persist in adulthood will only cloud that ability to *Discern* and take you off course. Don't get me wrong, selfishness may provide you with some temporary gratification that will lead you to believe that you are getting ahead; however, in the end that's not how it will pan out for you. So just keep in mind that children do *Discern* in a limited capacity. But as they grow into adults, they cannot continue operating in this limited capacity or that natural ability to *Discern* will become stifled and selfish desires will take over and dictate a very different outcome than expected. This, incidentally, is exactly how adults negate their ability to *Discern*. It all starts when we're young and it also starts with our environment and our choices. We need to think about what we're doing and why we're doing it. If we can't explain the 'why', then we need to rethink our decisions.

When we talk about children and *Discernment*, there are other things to also consider. For example, parents have a hard time understanding why children decide not to share with them certain information that the parent deems important but that the child does not want the parent to know. There may be multiple reasons why a child would do this, but one of the reasons why they do it is because they *Discern* how you will respond to the information and they decide that it's best not to say anything to you. Now, because they are children and they may not ultimately know what is best for them at the time, that decision is based upon information they know about you which makes them believe that telling you is not the right thing to do. But again, they are children and they do not necessarily know what is best for them. But understand that they are taking their cues from you and what you are showing them. A perfect example of how this plays out is when a child is having a problem with another child at school. Here is the situation:

Let's say you have a shy, quiet child who is cooperative and obedient inside and outside the home. Let's also say that another child at school decides he is going to bully this kid. Now the bullied child's personality may be one where he doesn't want any trouble and he is hoping the other child eventually leaves him alone. This same child, even though he may want the bullying to stop, may not want to tell his parents if he knows the parents will do one or all of the following: a) come up to the school to confront the child, b) contact the child's parents, c) involve the principal and d) basically do all the things that would absolutely mortify the child.

Now from the parents' perspective, they are only protecting their child. But from the child's perspective, that would be a nightmare. Knowing what these parents will do, what do you think this child would do? In this instance, the child may elect to suffer in silence instead of telling the parents about being bullied. Hopefully the child will at least tell an adult he trusts so that the issue can be addressed before it gets worse. But many times, things do get worse because the child does not want to be embarrassed nor does he want others to know he's being bullied. And if the parents find out about the bullying from another source other than the child, the parents become upset and can't understand why the child didn't say anything to them.

In this situation, parents fail to acknowledge how they may have contributed to their child's decision not to divulge pertinent information in the first place. The shy or timid child may decide not to provide the parents with information even though he may do this to his detriment. Again, children *Discern*, mostly to satisfy themselves, but they also *Discern* to make sense of their limited view of the world. And since they *Discern* from a child's perspective, they may not know how to obtain the correct outcome. This is why parents play a pivotal role in how children *Discern*. Remember, children are absorbing the information they receive from you and they process that information the best way they can. So, for example, if you as a parent show your child that you will fly off the handle in front of them and others during times of conflict, that child is going to use that information to determine what he will and will not share with you. Therefore, parents and any adults who work with children or who are around children, need to know that children *Discern* and they use the information you convey to them whether you intended to convey the information or not. The lesson here: Please be careful of what you say and do around children and know that they learn to *Discern* based upon what they see, hear and experience primarily from YOU and others you allow around them.

Chapter Fourteen

PROFESSIONAL DISCERNMENT

For the past six years, I've been teaching courses in business, ethics and leadership, entrepreneurship and social entrepreneurship. I enjoy teaching all of these courses. In particular, my business course is a course that teaches students how to start and sustain a successful business. My ethics and leadership course is taught to students at the graduate level and the topics are varied and captivating. The students in my classes run the gamut in terms of the types of people who come through the class. My classes span the diversity of baby boomers to millennials and everyone in between. With each course I teach, I am always amazed at the differences in opinions and approaches I encounter from students from different generations, backgrounds and cultures. I also find it interesting teaching a group of students 'How to Start and Successfully Sustain a Business' when a number of students in the class haven't even had a permanent full-time job because they've been in school all their young lives.

But regardless of where each student happens to be in their adult life, I always start off my classes by telling my students that one of the best skills they can use and develop, especially if they haven't done so already, is their individual ability to *Discern*. At the beginning of each class I incorporate exercises that help students develop their able to *Discern* in their personal lives and as a business owner because *Discerning* should take place in all aspects of your life.

When I first get to know my students, one of the first things I ask is this: "Why do you want to start a business." As you can imagine, the answers vary depending upon the person, but I always take particular note when someone tells me how they just can't work for someone else. They go on to tell me that they just haven't been able to get along with their bosses but they are rather vague on why this is the case. I then start to ask questions, the first one being, how many jobs have you had where you could not get along with your superior? This is a crucial question and depending upon the answer, red flags may be flying high.

If the person tells me that they couldn't get along with any of their bosses, then at some point the person needs to examine whether they are the problem and not the people they've worked for. Unfortunately, we do not like to think we are the problem or the source of tension that exists in our relationships, whether professional or personal. But without analyzing and understanding what was the problem with these employment relationships, it is dangerous to think the solution is to open your own business. It is quite possible that the same reasons why you couldn't get along with your prior bosses may be the same reasons why you cannot effectively get along with your potential employees, clients and other professional relationships you will need to establish as a business owner. Therefore, being fed up with your prior employment relationships without examining what caused the problems in the first place, is not a good foundation upon which anyone should go into business. However, you'd be surprised at how often people actually start a business on that premise only to ultimately fail. This is particularly alarming especially if the business idea is a great one. However, the overall business fails because of your failure to deal with your personal flaws that will hinder your progress in business. This is why I always tell students that they need to know who they are, understand what their strengths and weaknesses are and learn how to establish relationships. All of these things are important components of making a business venture successful.

DISCERNING AT WORK AS AN EMPLOYEE

For most of us, before we have a supervisory title at work or before we take the step of starting our own business, we start out as employees. And when it comes to professional relationships, some people will assign titles to people to signal the level of involvement they have with certain co-workers, i.e., acquaintances or associates. But placing a title on someone isn't the end all be all when navigating work relationships, especially when you have to spend a significant amount of time with your co-workers. You have to take into consideration what your goal is, where are you trying to go in the company, what the corporate culture is like, and of course, where you see your future in the company.

For example, take the relationships you form with co-workers. Your relationships with co-workers, just like any other relationships in your life, require you to *Discern* so that you can protect yourself and the Core Values you uphold. Nothing tests your Core Values like relationships, whether professional or personal. That's why you must be vigilant in standing firm on your beliefs and navigating your relationships in context.

Some people have to learn this the hard way, but I've said this plenty of times and I'll say it in this book: Individuals you work with should never achieve friendship status with you so long as you work together. Work relationships, just like landlord/tenant relationships, always have the potential to go south. Some people know this to be true, yet they still allow their emotions to take over and foolishly get involved with someone at work. If the work relationship is one in which one person is in some type of supervisory position over the over, that is a definite 'No!' But even if both employees are at the same level, there is a possibility that one person can get promoted over the other and then somehow the other person may feel a certain way. Next thing you know, the relationship takes a turn for the worse and a half-truth story emerges and threatens the person who's been promoted. And yes, there are always situations where an intimate relationship at work has a happy ending, but those tend to be the exceptions rather than the norm.

The same thing is true in landlord/tenant relationships. First of all, whether the tenant is family, friend or stranger, the landlord/tenant relationship is a business relationship. This is true even when you allow family to stay at a property you own and they are not paying rent. Do you know why? Because that property you own is an asset that appreciates over time. So whoever you allow to live in it needs to keep up the property so that this asset is protected. That's business. This is also why I always tell people that if you decide to rent out your house, you should never have to rely on the rent to pay the mortgage or any other bills for that matter. That rent should be extra income and you should be able to pay the mortgage without relying on the rent because there is always the potential for the tenant to stop paying. Always! If that happens, now you have a problem on your hands because the mortgage is due and your tenant of ten years just lost his job. It doesn't matter that this person has been the best tenant you ever had. The bottom line is, if that wonderful tenant cannot pay any longer and you relied on his rent to pay certain bills, you now have a situation on your hands. This is why you need to truly *Discern* when establishing these types of relationships. Plain and simple

DISCERNING AS A MANAGER

The stakes become even greater when you are placed in a position of authority. Being a manager requires you to *Discern* as you navigate different employees with different personalities and gifts while treating everyone equally. You will have a different level of responsibility as a manager so you must know how to lead. Being in this position requires you to know your strengths and weaknesses while motivating people to complete their jobs and respect your authority. There are plenty of times when people assume such authoritative positions without knowing their shortcomings or even knowing how to manage others. When that happens, the manager creates more problems than they can solve. This results in a problem with the employees they supervise and/or the superiors to whom they must report. Therefore, if you've assumed this position without the benefit of *Discerning* daily, it would behoove you to learn to do so immediately.

DISCERNING AS A SMALL BUSINESS OWNER

It's difficult for me to even think about someone opening up their own business if they're not *Discerning* on a regular basis. This is exactly why I start all of my business courses with several exercises designed to get the students to engage in the self-reflection they should be engaging in periodically. The goal is for you to get to know you on a deeper level. After we get to know ourselves better, I let the students know that there are four things a person should know before starting their own business. Here they are:

1 - Not everyone is your customer or client

One of the most valuable lessons to learn in business is the fact that not everyone is your customer or client. Only *Discernment* will make you aware of this fact. People who focus solely on the money will not understand this lesson until they regret having someone as a client. This is not how it should work, especially when you are providing services but this also applies to businesses in general. If you fail to plan or map out your business idea, you are already starting at a disadvantage. Things such as start-up costs, having the right advisers and consultants, having a budget and looking at long-term and short-term goals are critically important for any business. If you do not account for those things, you will start off your business playing catch up. This is not a good position to be in as a business owner. If you do not plan the business and instead rely on the fact that the business idea is great, you are being misled. You cannot let the money be the driving force behind who you allow as customers. Chasing the money will not alert you to the warning signs of a potential client who you can never satisfy, but *Discernment* will. I'll give you an example of how *Discernment* will help you in business.

When I first opened my law practice I made sure I did so after discussing it with my husband and making sure that we could either maintain our current lifestyle on his salary or we'd have to make some adjustments to that lifestyle and revise our budget to ensure that we implemented the appropriate measures for our family. After putting in the work, we determined that we could sustain our lifestyle on his salary which meant that any income I made would go towards savings. Other people who performed this analysis may determine a different outcome. For example, you may determine that a modest income from the new business is needed or perhaps you will need to cut back on a few luxuries for a certain amount of time until you can evaluate the effectiveness of the business. No matter what is determined, the point is that you must perform an analysis in order to know how to proceed. This is the position you want to be in when starting a business.

When we made our determination before opening my business, we knew where we stood financially. Also, getting over that hurdle allowed me to focus on client development and focus on *Discerning* what clientele I was looking to retain. That means my mind can focus on other aspects of the business and not have to take anyone who walks in the door. Remember, not everyone who walks through the door should be your client.

I can recall having a consultation with a potential client. After the consultation I informed the client what it would cost to retain my services. The potential client then hesitated and said to me 'well, I spoke with someone else yesterday and his price was about $1,000.00 less than what you just told me. I don't have that kind of money right now. I can give you the same amount the other attorney was going to charge me.' My first thought was 'You need to go back to that other attorney's office.' Of course I did not say this to the potential client. I did, however, stick to my price and informed him that it was firm. I do not haggle with my pricing. This isn't a pawn shop. But here is the most important part of this exchange: this potential client was actually telling me what type of client he would be. Right off the bat he was telling me that he would not pay me what I require. That is unacceptable. However, if I didn't do the work to know where I stood with the business and I was just focused on getting whatever money was waved in front of me, I would have taken on this client who clearly did not respect my time or expertise and who also tried to dictate what he was going to pay for my time. This is why planning is important. When you plan and know what your business needs, and more importantly, when you know your worth, you can *Discern* and decide how you will conduct your business and not let money blind you. If you do, you may end up with a client who will not pay your bills and cause you more grief than you bargained for. There are plenty of ways potential clients tell you that they should not be your client. You must *Discern* in business. Do not forego planning and do not focus solely on the money.

2 - Understanding your strengths and weaknesses

It is imerative that you know your strengths and weaknesses. This is part of the self-reflection process that helps you understand who you are and what attributes and qualities you bring to the business setting and what areas you need to improve upon. It will also help you identify the qualities you are looking for in other people, qualities that you lack. You need to write out your strenths and weaknesses. This is a great exercise that will help you become a better you. Dr. A. R. Bernard of the Christian Cultural Center in Brooklyn, New York spoke about accentuating your strengths and managing your weaknesses. I wholeheartedly believe in this statement. I believe that by managing your weaknesses, you acknowledge that they exist and you learn to keep them in check. I always tell my students that if you fail to acknowledge your weaknesses and deal with them, they tend to surface during the most inconvenient times, especially when you are running a business. That's why you need to admit to yourself if you are a control freak. Once you admit it, now let's deal with it; you can work on that aspect of your character, try to understand why you are that way and manage that weakness. And on the other side, highlight your positive attributes and determine how those attributes can be utilized for business purposes. This is why identifying your strengths and weaknesses is vitally important because it helps you *Discern* what areas of concern you will need to address based upon your strengths and weaknesses. And when I say identify strengths and weaknesses, I mean identify any areas or personality traits/qualities you have in general. Do not attempt to identify only those attributes you believe apply to the business. No. You need to think more broadly and list <u>ANY</u> strengths and weaknesses you have. Please take some time to write down your strengths and weaknesses in the chart below.

Strengths	Weaknesses

3 - You must know how to establish relationships

Here is one of the most important tips you should know about going into business: If you cannot establish and maintain relationships, you are dead in the water. The ability to maintain relationships is fundamental. Once again, this is why you need to know the type of person you are and how you get along with other people. This is also why I continue to probe my students if they tell me they could never get along with their prior employers. This is a serious red flag that must be dealt with immediately. Knowing when to burn a bridge with someone is a skill that one should only plan through *Discernment*. Knowing how to speak with and connect with all different types of people involves the ability to *Discern*. You need to understand this before you start a business because you do not want to bring the same old habits into your business, especially if you failed to deal with them. These destructive habits will suddenly make appearances as you attempt to develop clients, establish business relationships and put your business on the map. Learn how to establish relationships through *Discernment* so that your business can have a fighting chance at success.

4 - Learn to hire people you need and not people who are like you or people who are 'yes men'

Finally, *Discerning* means that you understand that your business needs a team of people who will compliment the business and who possess the experience and overall personality, work ethic and other traits to make the business flourish. Unfortunately, when we interview candidates, we are drawn to people who we feel are like us. It's the law of attraction. In other words, we are attracted to people who possess the same type of energy that we have. However, that's not what the business needs, especially if you are honest with yourself to determine that you do not possess all the qualities needed to run the business successfully. Therefore, you are actually looking for people who compliment you and possess the qualities you need for the business, but qualities that are not possessed by you. You also do not need to hire people who will only tell you what you want to hear instead of what you need to hear. This is true on a personal level as well, but I digress again. Do you see why all of these exercises of self-reflection, strengths and weaknesses, planning and a host of other tasks are important? *Discernment* should be involved from beginning to end when deciding to start your business before you actually open for business.

There are other lessons in business that are crucial to the success of starting a business venture. *Discerning*, of course, is at the top of the list along with the four topics we just discussed. If you are interested in starting a business, there are a number of outstanding books that I believe will help you get started. John Maxwell is one of the leading experts on leadership. I highly recommend any of his books and I particularly recommend his books and videos on the Five Levels of Leadership.

What you need to know is that learning how to *Discern* in a professional relationship is critical to professional success. There are enough books on business out there for you to know how to start a business.

However, *Discerning* is where you need to start. If you don't even understand when a relationship is a professional one and not a personal one, that will be a costly mistake for you. *Discernment* will stop you from making that mistake and, at the same time, *Discerning* will take your business to new heights. The lesson here: remember to invest in *Discerning* when it comes to business and you will ultimately be investing in yourself. The dividends will yield great results for years to come.

Chapter Fifteen

DISCERNMENT IN THE AGE OF SOCIAL MEDIA AND UNACCOUNTABILITY

I would be remiss if I completed this book without discussing the apparent absence of *Discernment* at the global level. The whole point of this book is for all of us to be cognizant of the fact that we need to *Discern* in life no matter what we are doing. Our circumstances should not dictate what happens to us. So if you have allowed your circumstances to dominate you up until this point in life, you need to make a commitment to change. Learning to *Discern* everyday should not be looked upon as a chore. If that is how you look at *Discernment,* then you are a big part of your problem. *Discerning* on a consistent basis should be the way you decide to live your life. In addition, because we live in a world that is constantly changing along with the culture, morals, values and ethics in society, you need *Discernment* to put it all into perspective and guide you along the way. If you commit to *Discerning,* you will find it to be the saving grace in your life.

Whether we are discussing politics, religion, sexuality, race or any other topic in between, technology has simultaneously opened doors and opened wounds in the world under the auspices that such technology creates a global community allowing people from all over the world to connect. That may have been the intended result, however, technology has unleashed an unprecedented number of platforms, the effects of which have manifest itself in destructive ways; these destructive ways will continue to impact people today, into the next generation and even beyond.

For example, Social Media has changed the landscape of how we communicate and interact with one another; but Social Media has also given us a bird's eye view into the unfortunate reality that too many of us are surviving in life and not actually living life. What do I mean by this? On the surface, it appears as if Social Media has provided a platform for us to express ourselves and become more conscious and educated about the world around us. However, with this platform also comes the other platform for those who seek to divide and conquer, spread hate and create dissention amongst certain groups of people. In that sense, Social Media beckons the coward to believe he or she is powerful by hiding behind words that are pointedly used to hurt and strike at everything that is wrong in society. These same people, although feeling powerful on Social Media, couldn't muster up the courage to say those words to an actual person if the opportunity arose. I'm speaking of those (commonly referred to as trolls) who roam the internet with the intent to provoke and never miss an opportunity to incite, degrade and denounce under a fake or less than truthful profile. That is classic cowardice.

Another problem with Social Media is that for far too many, it creates an illusion of happiness and fulfilment. This illusion is sometimes perpetrated by the one posting and other times it is perpetrated by the person viewing the post; sometimes it's both. These illusions are not limited to the ones posting and commenting. Plenty of times it also applies to those sitting on the sidelines viewing posts and internalizing Social Media content in a way that prompts a subjective reaction either on Social Media or in their private lives. This is dangerous, especially since there are scores of content posted on Social Media that are not rooted in fact and many people do not seek to verify the content before they respond or internalize the misinformation. Unfortunately, however, they respond because they feel a need to respond primarily because their response somehow gives them some sort of psychological satisfaction. So now the question we need to ask ourselves is: *why do we have a need to be validated through Social Media?*

This becomes a valid question if we truly take a look at our lives and examine the amount of time we spend on Social Media and further analyze the role it plays in our lives. But the reason why I broach the topic of Social Media and anyone's use of it in their life is because there is very little, if any, *Discerning* that takes place in the context of Social Media. Therefore, anyone getting caught up in the world of Social Media should examine why Social Media is necessary for them. At the end of the day, Social Media is not a bad thing; however, just like anything else we may get involved in, we need to determine if we are using it purposefully without allowing it to affect our psyche in ways that hurt more than help. Even further, we need to look at how our use of Social Media affects our loved ones including our children, our significant others, our friends and even our jobs.

Even if you are a responsible Social Media user, it is very difficult to manage your single responsible behavior in a sea of irresponsible behavior. This is why I believe that, generally speaking, Social Media is not a platform for productive, meaningful discourse or healthy debate. Even when you bring your level-mindedness and professional demeanor to a Social Media discussion, all it takes is for one comment to lower the discussion to a pissing contest. Participating in such discourse accomplishes nothing more than a psychological feeling of satisfaction similar to the one many of us feel when someone 'likes' our post. But again, the question is still: *why do you need this feeling and what purpose does it serve in your life?*

And if we go deeper into Social Media, we cannot ignore those who use Social Media to establish relationships. This is not about berating anyone for finding love in cyberspace; if it happens, great. However, Social Media is being touted by some as a valid way of establishing relationships with people. However, the fundamental problem with Social Media and relationships is that you don't know if the information being presented to you is fact. A 40-year old 4'9 foot tall brunette who weighs 185 pounds could use the picture of a twenty-two year old 5'7 blonde and you wouldn't know unless you meet them. And although you can *Discern* through online conversations, there is still a level of uncertainty that can only be clarified if and when you meet the person. Therefore, you accept a higher level of risk through Social Media until you are able to verify by way of a face-to-face meeting. This is exactly why you need to consider why and how you use Social Media.

Just so you don't think I'm totally against Social Media, you should know that I use Social Media. However, I have specific goals for both my personal and business Social Media accounts. My goals for both accounts are the same: to uplift, inspire and educate; the only difference between my personal Social Media and my business Social Media is the actual content displayed on each platform. Incidentally, my Social Media goals are consistent with what I believe is my true purpose in life.

With goals in mind, my use of Social Media is meaningful and requires me to make sure my goals are being met. I keep these same goals in mind if I find the need to respond to anyone's comments on my post; the same applies to any comments I decide to make on someone else's post. Overall, my use of Social Media will need to fit into my overall purpose in life and, therefore, I need to periodically examine whether I'm staying on track with this overall goal. This is also how you should proceed with Social Media as well. If your use of Social Media stirs up emotions within you that makes you step outside your goals, you need to take a step back and deal with why you feel the need to do this. You do not have control over what others say on Social Media. The only thing you do have control over is you and that's who you need to confront. The point is that your use of Social Media should be purposeful and consistent whether you are posting, commenting or responding. Here are some reflective questions you should think about for your Social Media platform:

REFLECTIVE QUESTIONS: USING SOCIAL MEDIA

1 - Do you use Social Media? If so, list the Social Media platforms you use?

_____
_____
_____
_____
_____

2 - Do you use Social Media for business, personal, or both? Do you have goals for both platforms? If so, list your Social Media goals for any platforms you have. If you do not have any Social Media goals, explain why not.

_____
_____
_____
_____
_____

3 - Do you comment on any Social Media or do you only comment on your posts? Explain why or why not?

_____
_____
_____
_____

. . .

4 - Explain why you specifically chose to use the Social Media platforms you decided to use. Do these platforms assist you with your social media goals?

_____

_____

_____

_____

_____

Hopefully, answering these questions will help you curtain your use of Social Media for a distinct purpose.

Finally, a major problem with Social Media is certain people's failure to take accountability for the misinformation they place out in the universe. This is why responding to a clever 'meme' that distorts an image/text for shock value or for a cheap laugh is a waste of time. You shouldn't get caught up in the web of unaccountability by validating it. Social Media should be handled from a position of *Discernment* so that you do not get caught up in unnecessary discourse that takes you further away from your goals and now places you in the circle of unaccountability with your response. Some people are purposely placing information out there just so you can have a reaction to it. You need to handle that from a position of *Discernment* the same way you would handle any other situation were *Discernment* is required. And with Social Media, more than likely, this means no response is required and you need to keep your emotions in check. If you know the truth about a particular topic and someone posts something on the topic that is an outright lie, let it go. You trying to set the record straight by responding to this person will not change a thing and now the person got what he or she set out to accomplish: getting you to stoop to his or her level. This is why you need to *Discern* as you use Social Media similar to how you *Discern* in the real world.

If you haven't already, start re-evaluating your use of Social Media and make sure it works for you. Do not allow Social Media to be another area in your life where you are being controlled and you're spending enormous amounts of time using it without it providing any measurable benefits to your life. Approach Social Media with *Discernment* in mind.

Chapter Sixteen
HOPE AND ULTIMATE DISCERNMENT

Speaking of Hope, it is my sincere hope that this book has answered any questions you may have about *Discernment* as well as broaden your understanding of what it means to *Discern*. The goal of this book is to educate, uplift and for all of us to think more logically and utilize the right information in making choices and life decisions. *Discerning* consistently makes us all realize that the power we have to change our lives for the better is a power that we all have inside of us. Using that power to its fullest potential will have a positive effect on ourselves, the people we care about, and the world if we do it consciously and purposefully. If we really want this to happen, we have to *Discern* regularly.

We must learn to use external sources for their limited purposes and not as a guide for our lives. Each of us already possesses a manual that is uniquely designed for our lives; the responsibility is for us to pick up that manual, follow the instructions and use it to fulfill our purpose in life. By no means am I suggesting that it is an easy task to accomplish. In fact, it is not easy. However, making a conscious effort to tap into this power is required so that you can focus on the right goals instead of nurturing bad habits and misguided energy. Again, being able to *Discern* does not mean that ALL the information is set before you; on the contrary, it means that the correct information is set before you. There is a difference! Waiting for all pieces of information to be presented to you before you act only gives you an excuse not to move. However, utilizing salient pieces of information is enough for you to make decisions and answer the call to action. When you are faced with situations that require you to *Discern*, you will know that you have all the information you need to move forward. If after reading this book you determine that you have not been *Discerning* as you make decisions, then start *Discerning* now. Review the questions in this book, look for the facts in every situation and get into the habit of self-reflection. I'm not a big advocate for creating habits, but if there are habits you should pick up, it is picking up the habits of self-reflection and *Discerning*. By doing so, you will discover how to make your life less complicated and more productive. You deserve better results and opportunities in life and *Discernment* will help you achieve maximum results.

Another important aspect of *Discernment* is something I touched upon in earlier chapters of this book. I am referring to the concept of hope and how we should find hope within the larger context of humanity and also the smaller context of improving our lives. We need to understand that many times hope is all we have. If we don't have hope, then we allow ourselves a cowardly 'out' when faced with difficult situations that require us to have more courage and faith. The possibility of hope should not only come up when we are in trouble. Hope should be beside you in life at all times like a tried and true friend. We don't always know when we'll need to rely on hope but if it is in the back of our minds as we walk this earth, we can find the good in situations where we didn't think it was possible. Having a solid belief in hope moves the mind and changes outcomes. It also keeps you in a positive frame of mind when the storms are threatening you and the hail is coming down hard on you. This is why as you *Discern* in life, the concept of hope should always be apart of the equation as you attempt to improve upon your existence in this world. The value of Hope and *Discernment* propels you to the highest level of conscious thinking and reasoning. Without hesitation, I can tell you that I aspire to achieve that level of consciousness and

Discernment has afforded me the opportunity to constantly re-evaluate my thinking.

I entitled this chapter 'Hope and Ultimate *Discernment*' because I find it necessary for you to understand that although some of you may be in the infancy stages of understanding and utilizing *Discernment* in your life, the far-reaching effects of *Discernment* are global. And let me be extremely specific in what I mean by this statement. There are some people in our world currently living and many people from our past who *Discerned* that their purpose in life was to sacrifice themselves for the greater good of the world. In other words, they knew they would die fighting for others. That, my friends, is what I call 'Ultimate *Discernment*'. Not everyone's purpose in life is to make that type of sacrifice. However, the ones who have determined that their purpose affects others on that level did so through their understanding of *Discernment* and Hope. You can see it by their actions and you can read it in the writings they left behind for us to study. Not only should we study their writings, but we should be inspired by them. I can think of a number of historical figures who fit this description. In particular, the first person that comes to my mind is Jesus Christ. And if you wanted to learn about the teachings of Christ and the sacrifices that he made, the Holy Bible provides a plethora of examples of how these sacrifices were made and its effect upon humanity. Another person that comes to mind on this topic is the Reverend Dr. Martin Luther King, Jr.

Ultimate *Discernment* comes into play when you have thoroughly and consciously examined your life to the point that you understand your purpose and how you are poised to affect millions of people. With this realization comes the fact that your life will be sacrificed in the process. Through *Discernment* you'll know the level of such sacrifice you are destined to make. But once you know what you're here to do, there is no turning back. Many people who are at this level of thinking don't turn back; they accept what is and begin to do the work.

Specifically, Dr. King comes to mind when I think about what he accomplished in the area of equal rights. He had a clear understanding of his purpose and how to live out that purpose. Everytime I read one of his many writings, and I do so periodically, I am able to understand his purpose and the ways he set out to fulfil that purpose. For example, I recently re-read the letter he wrote to clergymen as he sat in a jail cell in Birmingham, Alabama. The clergymen had criticized him over the methods he used to combat injustice. The letter he wrote was quite long and as I read it, I could see the vision through his words and how he *Discerned* what must be done. Here is just a small sample of what he wrote:

> "…. . I am in Birmingham because injustice is here. Just as the prophets of the eighth century B.C. left their villages and carried their 'thus saith the Lord' far beyond the boundaries of their hometowns, and just as the Apostle Paul left his village of Tarsus and carried the gospel of Jesus Christ to the far corners of the Greco Roman world, so am I compelled to carry the gospel of freedom beyond my own hometown. Like Paul, I must constantly respond to the Macedonian call for aid.
>
> Moreover, I am cognizant of the interrelatedness of all communities and states. I cannot sit idly by in Atlanta and not be concerned about what happens in Birmingham. <u>Injustice anywhere is a threat to justice everywhere. We are caught in an inescapable network of mutuality, tied in a single garment of destiny. Whatever affects one directly, affects all indirectly.</u>"[1]

Just by reading and comprehending this portion of the letter, it is clear that Dr. King knew his purpose in this world went far beyond his family, the community he lived in and even beyond the borders of the United States. He knew he had to leave his wife and children in order to preserve their freedom but he also knew that their freedom was connected to others. This man received daily death threats but he never allowed those threats to derail him and take him off course. He knew he was going to die and it didn't stop him from making ultimate sacrifices even though his children needed him as a father and his wife needed him as a husband. *Discernment* dictated that the world needed him more than his family did. Even in his 'I've Been to the Mountain-top' Speech, Dr. King spoke of not living long enough to witness all that he was fighting for; he knew and was at peace with not seeing the fruits of his work come to fruition when he stated:

> "We've got some difficult days ahead. But it really doesn't matter with me now, because I've been to the mountaintop. And I don't mind. Like anybody, I would like to live a long life. Longevity has its place. But I'm not concerned about that now. I just want to do God's will. And He's allowed me to go up to the mountain. And I've looked over and I've seen the Promised Land. <u>I may not get there with you. But I want you to know tonight, that we, as a people, will get to the promised land!</u>"[2]

He may not have known the exact date and time he was going to die but he knew his life would be cut short due to the work he was trying to accomplish and the hate that was consistently coming his way. He had already been stabbed prior to giving this speech. Someone else who didn't understand his true purpose in life may have stopped their work after being stabbed. But that's the beauty of Ultimate *Discernment* and Hope. The daily practice of *Discernment* carries with it 'Hope' and a deeper level of human consciousness that transcends fear, anger and all the other emotions that would stop one from moving forward. And even though Dr. King, in fact, did not live to see all that he worked for take shape, he planted seeds that are still growing today. The work he performed and the conviction behind his speeches are still taking flight and still resonate with people throughout the world. Generations and generations of people will be educated on the work of Dr. King because his life was a testament to how one person's vision can change the world. He led with love, respect, human dignity for all, kindness and hope. All of this was accomplished through *Discernment* which led him to a keen sense of understanding. How many of us today could imagine making sacrifices at that level?

My purpose in discussing Ultimate *Discernment* and Hope is not to say that you need to strive to make sacrifices on Dr. King's level. We all have different purposes in life that would require us to take certain steps in order to fulfil our specific purpose. I don't know what those steps would be for you. However, remember the *Discernment* Spectrum we discussed in Chapter Three? On one end of the Spectrum, you *Discern* and begin to open up new possibilities and opportunities for yourself and your loved ones. On the opposite end of the Spectrum, *Discerning* may involve decisions of life and death as it did with Dr.

King and others whose purpose pointed towards that end of the Spectrum.

It is your job to determine where you fall on the *Discernment* Spectrum. And the only way you will do that is to start *Discerning* so you can live the life you were meant to live but couldn't figure it out. *Discernment* is a huge part of the answer many of us have been looking for all our lives. The sooner you understand this, the sooner you can stop letting others maintain control over your life. That yearning you feel inside is real; it is *A Yearn To Discern* and it's calling your name. Tap into this internal element and start living the life you were meant to live. Your soul longs for it, your happiness depends upon it, your prosperity is counting on it and the world needs it. Start *Discerning* today and take your rightful place in this world. Whether you know it or not, that Yearn to *Discern* has been beckoning you all along. It's time for you to answer the call to *Discern*.

NOTES

1. THE ORIGINS OF THE WORD 'DISCERN'

1. Merriam-Webster.
2. Wikipedia.
3. yourdictionary.com.
4. Grace to You (gty.org).
5. christianitytoday.com.
6. Oxford Advanced Learner's Dictionary.
7. Wiktionary.
8. Etymology Dictionary.
9. Oxford Dictionary.
10. This may be confusing at first, but question five is a separate question for you to reflect upon. It's important to first be clear about the actual catalyst that prompted you to make a particular decision, whether that decision was influenced by people, circumstances or both. Once that is clearly determined, then you must be honest about the reasons or excuses you actually stated, either to yourself or to others, as to why you made your decision. If the reasons you gave at the time are different than the true reason why you made your decision, you need to be honest about it here. These questions are asked separately so that we can identify and discuss any inconsistencies or reasons why we handled the situations in a particular manner at that time.
11. Collins English Dictionary.

2. DISCERNMENT AND SPIRITUALITY

1. We will discuss the differences between *Discernment* and Intuition in a subsequent chapter.
2. Absent any neurological and/or developmental disabilities, the ability to *Discern* is possessed by all of us.
3. The Holy Bible, English Standard Version.
4. The Holy Bible, English Standard Version.

5. DISCERNMENT, CORE VALUES, PRINCIPLES & RULES

1. Oxford Dictionary.

6. LIFE LESSONS THAT SHAPE YOUR ABILITY TO DISCERN

1. 'Takers' is defined more fully in the Chapter entitled Relationship Discernment.
2. Dell Publishing 1997.
3. Merriam-Webster; Dictionary.com.

16. HOPE AND ULTIMATE DISCERNMENT

1. Except from a letter written by the Reverend Dr. Martin Luther King, Jr. as he sat in a Birmingham, Alabama Jail on April 16, 1963.
2. Excerpt from the 'I've Been to the MountainTop' Speech given by the Reverend Dr. Martin Luther King, Jr. on April 3, 1968.

ACKNOWLEDGMENTS

First and foremost, I acknowledge the presence of God in my life and God's work in me. I am thankful for each and every life experience I endured and the lessons I've learned along the way leading up to this book, which I believe God put on my heart to write. I will continue to be thankful for every day I'm given.

I am thankful for the family I was born into and all that I was taught through family. I am particularly thankful for my mom, my dad, my siblings and notably, my sister Alvina Rhea Johnson, and all that we shared. She is truly the inspiration behind this book and I know her spirit will live on through all that she accomplished and everyone she touched on earth. She is my Guardian Angel and I thank God for her.

I am thankful to my Publisher, Red Penguin Books, and specifically Stephanie Larkin, who understood the concept for this book from our first meeting. Our very first breakfast meeting lasted for over four hours and ended with a book deal. Stephanie saw the vision and relevance of this topic and I'm truly grateful for that.

I am thankful for the God-Given ability to *Discern* that has saved my life countless times. My goal is to continue to improve upon and sharpen this ability so that I may live purposefully and abundantly, not just for myself, but for others as well.

I am thankful to all the *Discerners* who came before me such as Dr. Maya Angelou and the Reverend Dr. Martin Luther King, Jr., whose words, actions and writings of Wisdom, Hope and *Discernment* continue to touch me and compel me to do better each and every day.

I am also thankful for those writers and leaders who think outside the box and who continue to dig deeper into human understanding and personal growth.

I am thankful for the teaching ministry of Dr. A. R. Bernard of the Christian Cultural Center in Brooklyn, New York. Dr. Bernard is the only person I know of who speaks of *Discernment*, good judgment and wisdom consistently and eloquently and whose teachings inspire me to walk by Faith and not by sight, sense or circumstance.

I am grateful to my friend, Gisela Ramos-Vega, who continued to send me words of encouragement and everything writing-related so that I could write my heart out.

I am thankful for my husband, Yves Maco, for being my audience/sounding board and always listening to my writing ideas. I am also thankful for Nia and Jazmin and our family dynamic. I treasure our family goals.

I am thankful for true friendships and, finally, I'm thankful that I'm still a work in progress . . .

ABOUT THE AUTHOR

R. L. Maco has a secret weapon–*Discernment*. It saved her life. Through *Discerning* consistently, she learned the value of making important decisions based upon facts instead of emotions. Being able to *Discern* properly is a skill that has shaped her adult life and propelled her to heights she never imagined in her youth.

Over the years, she's shared the benefits of *Discernment* with others and incorporated those benefits into her college course curriculums. Teaching students how to *Discern* in business and in life are critical components of the courses she teaches in business, ethics, leadership and entrepreneurship. Seeing how her teachings impacted her students greatly, she decided it was time to share her wisdom with a wider audience and wrote this book. Sharing the lessons she's learned through *Discerning* regularly has been one of the absolute joys of her life.

In addition to teaching, Maco is a successful practicing New York attorney with over 16 years of experience in litigation, business development and contract disputes, amongst other areas. Maco is also a recipient of the Reverend Dr. Martin Luther King, Jr. Humanitarian Award that was awarded to her by the County of Nassau, New York for her community service efforts. She lives in Baldwin, New York with her husband and their 2 daughters.

www.ingramcontent.com/pod-product-compliance
Lightning Source LLC
Chambersburg PA
CBHW072005110526
44592CB00012B/1211